Rollicking fun or elegantly chic — the enchanting
real-life wedding scenarios featured in this inspiring guide:

"All the Guests Wore White"   A backyard transformed into an
enchanted glade was the setting for a Gatsby-like lawn party
where every guest came in white. . . . Exquisitely beautiful,
incomparably romantic.

"Their Secret Garden"   At a charming, century-old inn with a
sunken rose garden, twenty-five guests discreetly gathered for
the ceremony before attending the hotel's regular Sunday "tea
dance" featuring a jazz-swing combo. . . . A delightful, virtually
cost-free wedding.

"How We Fell in Love Wedding"   Boarding a chartered bus
complete with professional driver, yummy hors d'oeuvres and
an excellent sound system, the guests and wedding party went
from the Irish pub where the couple first met to "their
places"—a Mexican Cantina and a fabulous downtown dance
club where the vows were said. . . . A great time, with great
memories.

"Caribbean Ceremony, Reggae Reception"   An "elopement" to
a hotel garden in the Bahamas avoided family frictions and
allowed a stress-free honeymoon before a homecoming
reception in a ballroom decked to nth degree with a Caribbean
motif. . . . A dream wedding for two people madly in love.

This imaginative planner will help you design a wedding—be
it elegant or whimsical—that celebrates *your* love, and honors
your values and uniqueness.

Creative Weddings

LAURIE LEVIN is a writer and a Ph.D. candidate in anthropology at the
University of California, Los Angeles. LAURA GOLDEN BELLOTTI is a
writer and the editor of such well-known books as *Women Who Love
Too Much* and *Letters From Women Who Love Too Much* by Robin Nor-
wood. They are co-authors of *You Can't Hurry Love: An Intimate Look
at First Marriages Over 40*. They both live in Los Angeles, California.

Creative Weddings

An Up-to-Date Guide for Making Your
Wedding As Unique As You Are

Laurie Levin and
Laura Golden Bellotti

A PLUME BOOK

PLUME
Published by the Penguin Group
Penguin Books USA Inc., 375 Hudson Street,
New York, New York 10014, U. S. A.
Penguin Books Ltd, 27 Wrights Lane, London W8 5TZ, England
Penguin Books Australia Ltd, Ringwood, Victoria, Australia
Penguin Books Canada Ltd, 10 Alcorn Avenue,
Toronto, Ontario, Canada M4V 3B2
Penguin Books (N.Z.) Ltd, 182–190 Wairau Road,
Auckland 10, New Zealand

Penguin Books Ltd, Registered Offices:
Harmondsworth, Middlesex, England

First published by Plume, an imprint of Dutton Signet,
a division of Penguin Books USA Inc.

First Printing, January, 1994
10 9 8 7 6 5

 REGISTERED TRADEMARK—MARCA REGISTRADA

LIBRARY OF CONGRESS CATALOGING-IN-PUBLICATION DATA:
Levin, Laurie.
   Creative weddings : an up-to-date guide for making your wedding as unique
as you are / Laurie Levin and Laura Golden Bellotti.
     p. cm.
   ISBN 0-452-27203-3
   1. Weddings–Planning. I. Bellotti, Laura Golden. II. Title.
HQ745.L46 1994
395'.22–dc20   93-31490
                                                      CIP

Printed in the United States of America
Set in Cheltenham Light
Designed by Eve L. Kirch

BOOKS ARE AVAILABLE AT QUANTITY DISCOUNTS WHEN USED TO PROMOTE PRODUCTS OR SERVICES.
FOR INFORMATION PLEASE WRITE TO PREMIUM MARKETING DIVISION, PENGUIN BOOKS USA INC., 375
HUDSON STREET, NEW YORK, NEW YORK 10014.

ACKNOWLEDGMENTS

We would like to thank

- our editor, Michaela Hamilton, whose timely idea it was to create a book for couples who want their weddings to go beyond the cliché. Her enthusiasm inspired us, and her support has been invaluable.

- our agent, Susan Schulman, who stands by us through thin and thick.

- all the grooms and brides we spoke to, who taught us that behind every wedding is boundless creativity, love, angst, and . . . a great story.

If a bride and groom want to do something their way, then I say, "Emily Post, get out of your grave and give me three good reasons why not!" *If a rule is going to make someone unhappy, then throw away the rule book.*

—Lori S. Jones, Current President of the
American Association of Wedding Directors

Contents

CHAPTER 1

Creative Couples, Creative Weddings

Breaking the Mold

Planning our wedding was the first chance we had to find out how we worked together. We had to decide how to present ourselves as a unified couple and still preserve our separate identities.

We wanted our wedding to be personal, sincere, and specific to our relationship. So we didn't do it the way it's always done, even though that would have been much easier. You know, the wedding gown, the tux, if the faces came off, it could be anybody. A wedding is deeply, deeply personal. If you put any thought or emotional investment into it, every aspect reflects you.

—Mark

I wanted some elements of tradition in my wedding, but I didn't want to feel like I was being sold to this man for life because I have a strong identity as a woman and think of us as equal adults. At the same time, I had a sentimental attachment to some of the bridal stuff, but I didn't want it to be like an adolescent prom ritual. So I tried to find a balance.

—Diane

All weddings celebrate the best of what life has to offer—love, passion, intimacy, and companionship. No matter how small or large, flamboyant or low-keyed, orthodox or off-beat, these joyful events symbolize the communion of two separate lives. For centuries, these ceremonies have been contained by a strict set of traditions and religious conventions. We first learn about the "cultural ideal" as soon as we are read our first fairy tale. From then on, a never-ending stream of images introduces us to the strict do's and don'ts of wedding etiquette. By the time we are grown, these images are deeply embedded in our consciousness.

"Perfect weddings" are defined by elaborate rules that explicitly dictate their form and content. Matrimonial road maps, otherwise known as wedding planners, can take you every step along the way, along the same path as everyone else. These planners leave no details to chance. Everything is codified. From how many ushers escort the mother of the bride to her seat to who reads the congratulatory telegrams and in what order. But what do you do if the advice from etiquette books doesn't fit your circumstances, beliefs, or values?

Well, move over Martha Stewart, Emily Post, and Amy Vanderbilt. Weddings are changing. Increasing numbers of newlyweds-to-be have taken matters into their own hands and are liberating themselves from the stifling confines of bride magazines and wedding expos. Instead of collapsing under the pressure to follow "wediquette" to the letter, many couples are adapting and reshaping traditional wedding ritual to reflect their own personal values, individual preferences, and life circumstances.

Time-honored conventions are being renovated to harmonize more closely with today's realities. Prescriptions governing rites, rituals, and roles are no longer being taken as gospel. Good examples are the customary profile and conduct of the bride and groom. Traditional wedding protocol assumes that newlyweds are young, never-married, and childless. But, as we all know, these assumptions may not necessarily be true. A great many first-time brides and grooms have deferred matrimony until their late twenties, thirties, and beyond. And, surprisingly enough, according to the Advance Report of Final Marriage Statistics, 1988 (National Center for Health Statistics, 1991), the most recent figures indicate that only 54 percent of all weddings unite brides and grooms who are both never-married. That means that the remaining percentage involves couples in which one or both newlyweds are remarrying. Still other "exceptions to the rule" are spouses-to-be who are single parents or have children from a previous marriage.

Furthermore, standard wedding rites fail to make allowances for other complexities of modern-day mate selection. A bride and groom may not be of the same faith or race. Nor do they automatically share the same cultural background.

Traditionally, most wedding decisions are made and executed by the bride and her mother, while the groom is relegated to the sidelines. But this exclusive domain is changing, too. More men are taking greater interest and participating more fully in every aspect of wedding planning.

Because life no longer fits into neat, predictable patterns the way it used to, wedding experts are flooded with queries from exceptional couples trying to get a reading on what is "socially correct" in these times of social change. The following excerpt from a popular wedding-advice column in *Modern Bride* (Oct./Nov. 1991, p. 28) regarding the wording of invitations is a good case in point:

> *Question:* I am a feminist and very uneasy about addressing the wedding invitations using the husband's first name. Is there an alternative to that?
>
> *Answer:* Despite your feminist predilections, it is socially appropriate to address the invitations in the traditional manner: Mr. & Mrs. John Smith, unless the wife has retained her family name (most people expect that on a formal invitation). Another exception is if the wife has a professional title. For example, if she is a physician the envelope would be addressed to Dr. Jane Smith.

This brisk response is hardly helpful, and not a little bit condescending. It leaves the bride few alternatives but to follow narrowly defined protocol. Moreover, the underlying message seems to be "stick to the rules or else!"

What if you are a remarrying bride who wants to wear full bridal regalia? Or part of an interfaith couple intent on blending your religious traditions into one ceremony? Or a remarrying dad whose children have special roles in your wedding ceremony? Or a groom who wants to have as much say-so in the "bridal" registry as the bride?

Must you succumb to outdated etiquette for the sake of convention? Creative couples who have planned creative weddings say *no!* They take the opposite tack and insist that *your wedding is for you, so don't let anyone tell you how to run it!*

Creative weddings are crafted as much by instinct as by imagination—not by "shoulds" or "musts." Deciding to break the mold, gives you the freedom to "mix and match" traditional elements with novel ones, with an emphasis on what pleases *you,* not the wedding experts. Think about it this way. You've chosen your mate. You've chosen to marry. Does it really make sense to plan the most unforgettable day of *your* life according to *someone else's* rules?

Perfectly Unpredictable Weddings

Creative weddings honor everything that traditional weddings do, and more: playful exuberance, whimsy, teamwork, decisiveness, diplomacy, improvisation, compromise, and a sense of humor. And the creative couples who plan them take as few or as many liberties with "wediquette" as *they* see fit and without worrying about what others will say. Not only do they know their own minds, they mastermind their own one-of-a-kind weddings!

Some examples: Mark and Leslie wanted an elegant wedding that wasn't stuffy or stolid. They rented an estate with ample grounds and facilities to match their ambitious plans. By day, the ninety guests swam, picnicked, and played volleyball and croquet. By night, all reassembled for a candlelight interfaith wedding ceremony, followed by a sit-down dinner and dancing to a Texas swing band.

Eileen and Ken envisioned something more conventional, but shook up the status quo when it came to who-did-what. Instead of divvying up their wedding work by tradition, they did it by talent. The result: a nearly total role reversal. All the major decisions for the traditional church wedding were shared. But it was Ken who coordinated everything from the bridal registry to picking out the dresses for the bridesmaids!

Charlotte and David discreetly staged their small ceremony, on a tiny budget, in the sunken rose garden of a renovated *fin de siècle* hotel without the staff even noticing. Twenty-five guests and a judge clustered around the couple while they took their vows. Once the ceremony concluded, the wedding party strolled back to a reserved room to feast and fete at the hotel's weekly Sunday Buffet Brunch and Tea Dance.

Mark and Leslie, Eileen and Ken, and Charlotte and David all preserved certain elements of traditional wedding etiquette and invented others. In still another departure from traditional wedding etiquette, they, like most of the other creative couples you will read about, planned and financed their weddings jointly. Among their many sound reasons for doing so are the following.

Paying for your own wedding theoretically gives you the right to plan and control what you want. The reasoning is only logical: if someone else is footing the bill, it's going to be more difficult for you to call the shots. Moms and dads, even if they are willing to finance the festivities, and many these days cannot, don't always share the same vision as their sons or daughters. Sometimes, these differences can lead to bickering and tension. By taking financial charge, brides and grooms can minimize these family flare-ups. Other couples who are older or remarrying feel that, as adults, paying for their wedding is their responsibility—pure and simple.

Because weddings have become extremely expensive, sharing the costs might be the only way a couple can afford one. The mushrooming bridal industry is now a thirty-one-billion-dollar-a-year business, and, according to an article entitled "Avoiding the Wedding Bell Blues" *(Changing Times,* April 1991), today's average wedding costs between $13,310 and $19,000, depending upon its location. At these prices, a couple must seriously consider whether one day of wedding bliss is worth mortgaging their future for and, if so, on whose terms.

The Lessons of Love

All weddings are a creative act. Few other events in our lives symbolize such a profound transformation. Even fewer hold as many hopes and dreams for the future. With so much attention and the highest of expectations riveted on "The Most Important Day of Our Lives," it is easy to forget that these few hours really celebrate an ongoing process, one that begins long before the actual "wedding day" and extends years beyond it.

As wonderful as weddings are, planning one isn't always the idyllic process we dream or read about. The practical side of wedding planning is a test of perseverance: nailing down a budget, selecting a site and date, deciding on the guest list and invitations, lining up the officiant(s), booking photographers and videographers, coordinating the food, drinks, entertainment, music . . . the details are endless.

Planning a wedding is also a test of diplomacy. As you have probably already noticed, the moment you announce your wedding to the outside world, the pressure is on. Advice—mostly unsolicited—comes pouring in. Suddenly, everyone has an opinion about everything—from who you *must* invite to the number of tea roses in the bridal bouquet. The question becomes how to hold your ground without permanently alienating those who are convinced they'd know how to plan your wedding better than you do!

Amid the avalanche of good intentions and exciting decisions, a far more subtle process is quietly taking place: the inner wedding. A truly "perfect wedding" is not simply the external event, but rather an emotional bonding of two people that potentially lasts a lifetime. In her book, *On the Way to the Wedding* (Boston: Shambala, 1986), Linda Leonard describes this most fundamental aspect of wedding.

> A wedding requires no less than a personal transformation . . . Many of us have had formal weddings and marriages which lacked the mystery of transformation. We have had the illusion of a wedding, the physical external ceremony, but not the inner spiritual uniting with the mysterious other. Some of us have given up on the wedding ritual for this very reason—it seems to have trivialized the most meaningful of events. We have mistaken the external ceremony for the inner event.

Preparation for the "inner wedding" often intensifies during a couple's engagement, whether it is a formal one or not. In social terms, this transitional period occurs between the time of being single lovers and being "husband and wife." "Fiancés" are accorded a special role in our society: recipients of much attention, fussing, and gentle teasing—all in anticipation of their new married status. In personal terms, spouses-to-be are sorting out their respective identities as separate individuals and as a couple. This delicate process intensifies as the wedding date approaches.

A wedding brings the complex backgrounds and psychologies of two individuals into intimate proximity. For the majority of brides and grooms, organizing a wedding is the *first* and most significant joint effort they have attempted together, replete with every imaginable as well as never-imagined emotion! About-to-be-married couples report being stressed-out, giddy, excessively weepy, gloriously compromising, monstrously obsessive, uncharacteristically snappy, and impossibly possessive.

Discussions about the human side of wedding planning are conspicuously absent in bridal books and magazines. The glossy images of "flawless" weddings impeccably executed provide us with false impressions about what we can expect when we plan one. The great temptation is to regard wedding planning simply as a means to an enchanted end. Yet, in many ways, it is the dress rehearsal for the marriage to come. Issues relating to money, control, decision-making, and the fear of change, to name only a few, often surface during the planning of a wedding. These conflicts are painful, but they can teach us about ourselves, our spouse-to-be, and our strengths and weaknesses as a couple. Couples who realize this, like the ones in this book, make a conscious commitment to grow and learn from the task before them.

Planning a wedding not only awakens our inner resources to deal with these differences, it also primes a couple for the real exchange and compromise that are essential in a successful marriage. If you pay close attention to the planning process, you can learn valuable life lessons: neither weddings, nor the very human being you are marrying, is perfect; if you expect them to be, you miss the essential point of love.

Beyond Wedding Etiquette

In celebration of your wedding, please accept this gift: the encouragement and inspiration of the creative couples who have planned their own creative weddings. In this book, they invite you to share the real stories of their celebrations, from the inception to the receptions.

As their special behind-the-scene guest, you will be privy to what few of their friends or family members may ever know— the fantasies and the finagling, the glitches and the goofs.

Learn that each wedding is as much a sacred journey as it is a labor of love, as you envision and plan yours.

Each wedding is the unique collaboration of a bride and a groom, as distinct from one another as they are from every other couple. So, too, are the creative couples you'll meet in the following chapters. As a group they represent varied backgrounds, races, occupations, ethnic groups, and faiths. Their ages range from mid twenties to early fifties. Some were marrying for the first time, some for the third. Some were childless, others had children, others were about to become stepparents. A number are interfaith or intercultural couples who are blending their beliefs and traditions. Others found more meaning and inspiration in creating their own ritual. With wedding budgets that ran the gamut from extravagant to spare, the majority of our couples paid for their weddings themselves. And, in just about every case, both the bride and groom planned the wedding together.

Unlike the majority of standard wedding planners, *Creative Weddings* is organized by wedding themes. If you look at the Contents you won't find generic topics such as invitations, attire, florists, videographers, and such. (For quick reference on these specific subjects, simply consult the Index.) Two or three unique wedding stories, from both the bride's and groom's perspective, form the centerpiece of each chapter.

The experiences of our creative couples reveal the inner workings of how real people make real wedding plans. Each account offers specific insights about aspects of decision making including:

- Envisioning a creative wedding
- Who plans what and who does what
- Finding and selecting the wedding site
- Cost-cutting strategies
- Sorting out the guest list and designing distinctive invitations
- Finding an officiant(s) and writing vows
- Defining the role of children

- Alternative gifts and the bridal registry
- Dealing with prewedding tension
                    ... and more

If "wedding" means the act of uniting separate beings in a sacred search for meaning in their lives, then those who craft their own celebration according to their own meaning deserve a hearty toast! You are destined to be among them and so we offer our most heartfelt congratulations. For there is no doubt, you are on your way to a most creative wedding.

~

Wedding Work: An Equal Opportunity

HELP WANTED: Take-charge, detail-oriented couple to design, organize, and pull off the most meaningful event of your life. Creativity, budget management, and personnel skills essential. Ability to work under pressure and deal diplomatically with pushy vendors and anxious in-laws a must. Working knowledge of the catering, floral, clothing, music, photography, and videography industries preferred. No pay, but fringe benefits include a rewarding experience and a priceless opportunity.

~

M any of today's grooms and brides are deciding that they *want* the job of creating their own wedding. The era in which mother-of-the-bride and her bride-to-be daughter make all the arrangements according to established wedding etiquette is being eclipsed by a new generation of couples who want to share in the planning of their day. Still, it's an enormous undertaking—and a "job" at which few couples have experience.

Even those who opt for small, simple weddings face dozens of organizational, financial, and aesthetic decisions. There's no getting around it—your wedding is a uniquely special event that requires a lot of work. But it's also one of the happiest days in a couple's life, and working together to create it can be exhilarating and fulfilling.

Planning a wedding with your husband- or wife-to-be is usually an intense learning experience as well. Couples must figure out—sometimes for the first time in their relationship—how to function as a team and accomplish a common goal. Such a momentous joint undertaking can be the source of considerable conflict. Sometimes without even being aware of it, the bride or groom has difficulty sharing the role of wedding CEO and wants exclusive control over all decisions. Conversely, one person might be overwhelmed with work and feel that the other isn't pulling their weight. Adapting to your partner's "style"—whether it be their approach to organizing or their manner of resolving conflicts—is the beginning of a process that will continue throughout your marriage.

Planning your wedding can also be an opportunity to build other relationships. It may be the first chance a bride has to really get to know her father-in-law; a groom may receive a crash course in his fiancée's family politics; or a bride/stepmother-to-be may begin to form a special bond with her new stepdaughter by including her in the fun and excitement of planning the wedding.

Timing and schedules was another frequently raised issue by the grooms and brides we talked with. A number of them told us they wanted to participate equally in the planning of their wedding, but unforeseen circumstances at work meant their partner had to take up the slack. Usually spouses-to-be took such unavoidable changes in stride, aware of workplace realities.

Some couples divided up responsibilities according to what they did best or what they most enjoyed; others were intent on sharing every facet of decision making. Sooner or later everyone acknowledged the importance of *delegating*—getting help from either family, friends, or paid professionals. You'll read a lot about this in the stories to follow.

In discussing how much time was required to plan their weddings, the couples we interviewed varied greatly—from one week to seventeen months! Although every bridal magazine includes a "bride's timetable," mandating that X amount of months before the wedding you *must* complete your guest list, have a preliminary dress fitting, finalize the reception menu, and such, we believe that planning your wedding can be much more flexible, depending on the style, size, and location of your event. Use those timetables just to get an idea of the many details involved, but don't be overwhelmed by them. Flowers don't always have to be ordered six months before the wedding, and there are plenty of musicians who don't need to be booked a year in advance!

There is, however, one unbendable rule when it comes to scheduling: Reserve the site for both ceremony and reception as soon as you set the date. Hotels, public buildings, and churches are often booked up to a year or more in advance.

Magazines and wedding etiquette books are also famous for their "separate and unequal" list of duties for the groom— usually limited to such "masculine" tasks as purchasing the ring and making honeymoon arrangements. We feel it's time the bridal industry woke up to the fact that grooms and brides have changed over the last twenty-five years. Many men want to be as involved as their fiancées in planning a day that is equally meaningful to them. And women are every bit as adept at making hotel and plane reservations as their male counterparts!

In this chapter we'll meet three couples, each with very different planning styles. Ken and Eileen's church wedding and hotel reception benefited from Ken's organizational savvy and Eileen's managerial skills; he was in charge of the details whereas she oversaw the big picture. Carl and Cynthia, equally involved in creating their unique hilltop ceremony and forest knoll reception, hired a wedding coordinator to augment their efforts. Matt and Nancy considered their backyard potluck wedding a family affair; bride and groom had veto power, but many family members pitched in to assure an unforgettable day. In each case, the question of "Who does what?" was resolved to accommodate the preferences, schedules, and personalities of both bride and groom.

The Groom Who Loved Details: Eileen and Ken

The Bride: Age 25, first marriage; six-year-old daughter from a previous relationship

The Groom: Age 27, first marriage

Ceremony: Lutheran

Site: Church ceremony, hotel reception

Guests: 200

Cost: $14,000

Eileen:
Ken is a full-service man. He's done absolutely everything except choose my dress and try it on for me. He's got a budget on the flowers, he's got the DJ, the cake, the place where we're having the reception,

the church. He knows where the tuxedos are coming
from, all of this is settled already—and the wedding
is still nine months away! He even asked me if I
wanted him to purchase the bridesmaids' makeup and
pantyhose . . . And I said, "Pantyhose???"

Ken:
   Okay. Let's get some background here. I was raised
by a woman . . . who had female friends . . . who had
daughters. And she raised me to be what she would consider
the perfect man. So as a result, I know how to do
a lot of things that most men don't. And it helps.

Nine months before their wedding, we asked Eileen and
Ken if they could give us a rough estimate of how much they
were planning to spend. Ken excused himself for a moment to
consult his files, returned to the kitchen table, and responded
down to the penny! From that moment on, we knew we were
dealing with an organization man par excellence.

Ken comes by his talent with numbers honestly—his background is in accounting. But far from being rigid or stuffy, he
has an exuberance and sense of humor that is infectious. And
so does his bride-to-be, Eileen, an office manager who could
moonlight as a dynamite stand-up comic if she so chose. They
approach their big day with both a sense of delight and level-
headedness. Working diligently to pay for their own wedding,
they're putting in overtime and carefully budgeting their two
moderate incomes to save the needed $14,000. All this at a
time when the economy is making it difficult for most people
to save anything at all. Eileen is one of seven daughters, and
Ken comes from a single-parent family, so both knew early on
that the expense of their wedding would be their own responsibility. And they've taken it on with pride.

During our interview with Ken and Eileen, we became fas-
cinated by how their planning skills are completely different
and yet mesh so well. Ken pays meticulous attention to specifics. His wedding card files, charts, and computerized lists are

beyond impressive. (We would feel confident hiring him to organize *anything!!*) Eileen, on the other hand, is more comfortable conceptualizing, stepping back and envisioning the event
as a whole. Ken described how they work together:

> *It sounds lopsided, but it isn't. There's a lot of discussion*
> *between us. Primarily about the big picture. Eileen*
> *paints the big picture for me, and then I make sure*
> *we get from point A to point B. I just want her to have*
> *the wedding she's always had in her mind.*

Ken has a system for everything—guaranteeing that no detail will be overlooked. In the middle of our interview, he
popped out of his seat, smiling proudly.

> *Let me show you something. These are our filing cards.*
> *Each prospective guest has a card, with their address,*
> *where they're sitting at the reception, gift received,*
> *description of the gift, thank-you note sent, etc. I also have*
> *a cash flow chart showing how much money we'll be*
> *spending each month, all the way up to the wedding.*

"He looked at a book on planning your wedding to see if he
had forgotten anything, but he could have *written* the book,"
Eileen added.

Was Eileen surprised when Ken took it upon himself to attend to most of the wedding details?

> *I was pleasantly surprised, because I saw three of my*
> *six sisters tear their hair out planning their weddings.*
> *They had husbands who weren't at all involved.*
> *Basically the guys just said, "Tell me where to stand."*
> *But the moment Ken proposed, he took the ball and started*
> *running with it. And I was like, "Great, now I don't*
> *have to do this." I dreaded thinking of all the planning*
> *and all the stress. As a matter of fact, the theme for our*
> *wedding is "No stress."*

Eileen and Ken felt that giving themselves 17 months to plan the wedding was the best way to cut down on stress. Ken explained:

With enough time to investigate who you're dealing with, you have the leeway to stick to your budget. You sit down and say, "Okay, this is going to cost this much." Then when you walk into a flower shop or a hotel and say, "I want to pay this much and if you're not willing to do it, we can go elsewhere," you know you have that extra time to shop around.

Ken and Eileen believe that being in control of their own wedding, rather than having family members call the shots, also reduces tension. Eileen was particularly concerned about her sisters' input:

My mom's passed away, but I have six sisters who are like mothers, so I could conceivably have six "mothers" mothering over me prior to this wedding. Ken and I made it very clear to them that we're paying for it, we're making the choices, and we're gonna suffer the consequences.

Ken concurred:

We didn't want the whole thing to mushroom into a big catfight. That's definitely not the way I wanted to enter into a new family. And my mom might have taken over too, in which case I would have had to watch her lose one hair at a time. So one of the ways we're avoiding stress is by taking charge of everything ourselves. It may not be perfect—the wedding may not start on time, the cake might fall, the limo might not show up—but at least we won't have too many cooks in the kitchen.

That doesn't mean, however, that they haven't asked sisters, brothers, and parents to take on certain tasks. "We are definitely into delegating," Ken insisted. For example, one of Eileen's sisters has excellent penmanship, so they talked her into addressing the invitations. Another sister is going to keep track of the gifts. And Ken's mother would have felt left out if she didn't have an important role, so they asked her to make the bridesmaids' dresses. Ken and Eileen also made a special effort to include Eileen's six-year-old daughter, Jennifer, in the planning process. They asked her to leaf through bride magazines and help find a pretty dress for her mom, and Ken consulted with her on favorite flowers for table decorations. Their rule of thumb was to pick the most qualified people for the jobs and give them enough time to carry them out.

Unlike many other couples we interviewed, Eileen and Ken had no problem striking the proper balance between delegating responsibility and retaining control. Many others who either couldn't afford a wedding coordinator or insisted on doing everything themselves, told us they regretted not calling upon friends and family to perform the myriad of large and small jobs with which they were saddled. Nine months prior to their wedding, Ken and Eileen had already anticipated and filled every conceivable personnel need.

In line with their policy of planning ahead, Eileen and Ken reserved the church early on (Ken is a member), and the two began to discuss their ceremony. There was a bit of conflict at first, because Eileen isn't religious and Ken is. She liked the idea of a church wedding but wanted a more "generic" ceremony that celebrated their union without "asking God's permission." Ken had to remind her that marrying in a church without mentioning God was not going to be possible. After some discussion with the minister, a compromise was struck. The Lutheran church to which Ken belongs is very liberal, and the ceremony will incorporate the couple's personally composed vows as well as the essential elements of the Lutheran service.

Deciding on the secular part of their celebration wasn't as controversial, and again Ken and Eileen were prepared well in advance. They chose the songs they'll be dancing to at their reception months ahead of time. Ken explained his choice:

> *Traditionally, the father dances with the bride—and Eileen will dance with her dad to "Unforgettable" by Natalie and Nat King Cole. But at our wedding, my mother will also dance with me. For that dance we'll play "Killing Me Softly" by Roberta Flack since it's the song my mother used to sing to me when I was a baby—and the first song I recognized.*

Because they each have only one parent, and since they're paying for the wedding themselves, they had a problem figuring out how to word the invitations. According to wedding etiquette, the bride's parents host the wedding and therefore their names appear first on the invitation, followed by the name of their daughter and then the man she's marrying. Eileen and Ken are hosting their wedding themselves but didn't want to offend their parents by not including them on the invitation. Then another complication arose. They wanted to name both Eileen's father and Ken's mother, but were afraid it might sound as if the two were a couple. Naming them separately appeared too wordy. They finally decided on the following compromise: "Together with their parents, Eileen and Ken request the honor of your presence . . ." That way their parents are acknowledged, but it's clear that the bride and groom are hosting their own wedding.

Although Ken's mother is making the bridesmaids' dresses, it was Ken who chose the pattern. Again, a male's involvement in an aspect of wedding planning usually reserved for females piqued our interest, so we asked Ken about it. He responded:

> *I got interested in all of this from watching other people's weddings and seeing how disappointed some of my friends were. I'm an incurable romantic and want Eileen to have the wedding she's always wanted. But when you start adding up all the numbers and realize*

that the cost is equal to a nice family car or a down
payment on a home, you don't want to make that
kind of investment in something that's going to be
a complete flop—or even a partial flop.

But how did he know about bridesmaids' dresses?

We saw this dress in a magazine, and it fits all the
qualifications. One bridesmaid is five foot one and
weighs 175 pounds, another is pencil thin. One is
extremely top heavy and a few are bottom heavy with
nothing on top. So this dress, I'm convinced, will be flattering
for all of them.

As he explained his thinking on the subject, Eileen started
laughing, "He gets into all of this, and I'm going, 'What's the
big problem? Just slap the dress on them!' "

They good-naturedly razz each other about their aptitudes
and interests, which definitely put sexual stereotypes to rest.
She's the one, for instance, who attends to car problems; he's
the cook in the family. On a recent trip to a department store
bridal registry, their lack of traditional sex roles baffled at least
one clerk. It seems reverse sexism reared its ugly head. Eileen
explained:

We went in and the guy sat us down and proceeded to
look at me the entire time. So he's explaining this and
that policy to me, and what merchandise they had,
and I'm just spacing out, thinking, "Let's see, Saturday
I'm going to be doing this . . ." I could have cared less
about what he was saying. It's Ken who cooks—he's
the one who turns out the fabulous meals. Then the
guy asks me to sign all these forms and Ken pipes in,
"Do you want me to sign anything?" and the clerk just
waves him away, "Oh, no, no." So then he says, "Okay,
now we're gonna walk around the store. Let me show
you the fine china, and these appliances . . ." Well, by

*the time we got to about the third section, he looks at
me and says, "You don't cook, do you?" And I said, "No,
I don't. You need to be talking to him!" pointing to
Ken. So the rest of the time the two of them chatted,
going through the whole list of stuff, occasionally asking
me whether I preferred Braun or Krups or something. But
it was really hysterical, because everything is geared
toward the woman, and yet it's Ken who knows what
he wants in the kitchen!*

Ken also found himself in a "no-man's-land" when he accompanied Eileen to the bridal salon. The personnel in the
shop were somewhat dismayed by his presence, relegating
him to a bench outside the shop! Ken had this to say about
how he was treated:

*It wasn't that I didn't realize I wasn't supposed to see
the dress ahead of time, but at what point do we start
looking at the bride and groom as a couple, at the
unity of it all. If the groom is there, at least respect that.
Offer him some coffee or something! I think people ought
to start giving more consideration to the groom. If he's
interested, he should participate. More important, this
is a couple's first step into a larger realm—how they're
gonna work things out together.*

We think Ken is simply ahead of his time. More and more
grooms are taking an active role in co-planning the big event
with their brides. It's the wedding industry that needs to get
hip to the fact that not only do today's men cook and clean,
they are also quite capable of—and interested in—making social and aesthetic decisions. If only we can begin trusting
them to do so.

When we asked Ken and Eileen what they had learned
about each other in the process of planning their wedding,
Ken answered thoughtfully,

*Eileen's enormous ability to trust me. She gives me a concept
and the freedom to say "I think it needs to go this way"
or "We need to shift it that way . . ." And she's okay
with it. I feel good that she's willing to trust me with
something that's so important to her. She's essentially saying,
"I trust you to make my dreams come true."*

Eileen learned that she and Ken are "very powerful together. Because he's 'A' and I'm 'B'—and when you put the
two of us together, it's a very strong link."

Tips from Eileen and Ken

1. Talk to each other. Tell the other person what you want
    to get out of this day, listen to what they want, and then
    incorporate what you both want.

2. Allow yourselves enough time to plan. You can save
    money and avoid stress by affording yourselves ample
    time to research prices and schedule necessary tasks.

3. Define the tasks you're each comfortable with, irrespec-
    tive of sexual stereotypes. One person's strength benefits
    the other and vice versa. It's not a competition.

4. Take your fiancé(e) with you when you buy the
    ring—to avoid spending a lot of money on something
    she/he may not like.

5. If you can do it, spend as much as you want if it makes
    you both happy.

And last but not least:

6. Don't pay too much attention to other people's advice.
    Once you tell friends and family you're getting married,
    everyone wants to give it to you! They'll have something

to say about everything! Take what applies to you and ignore the rest!!

Produced and Directed by Us: Cynthia and Carl

The Bride:	Age 30, first marriage
The Groom:	Age 39, first marriage
Ceremony:	"New Age" Jewish
Site:	Mountaintop ceremony, forest grove reception
Guests:	150
Cost:	$20,000

Carl:
*Our wedding was a "production" in the literal sense.
Detail was important to us, to plan this thing from
soup to nuts. It didn't feel like an obsessive thing or an
ego thing, it was simply something we wanted to do right.*

Cynthia:
*We had lists in the computer: hotels, guests with
problems, even a list of two hundred songs for the DJ
to find.*

They're both employed in the film business, so it was natural for Cynthia and Carl to equate the planning of their wedding to a film "production," with their roles being co-producer and co-director. Like their movie counterparts, one of their first joint decisions was selecting a location. That was the easy part—they both knew they wanted to be married on a mountaintop. It was a place that held a special significance for them as a couple. Not only has Cynthia led and filmed mountain treks, but "the mountain location was symbolic of a very important part of our relationship," she recalled.

> Carl climbed the highest peak in Europe with me, and it was a symbolic turning point for us. When he did that, he put his life on the line literally, and it was almost as though there was no turning back in the relationship after that.

Since Mt. Tamalpais (in Marin County, California) had been a sacred place for Native Americans, the two felt it would be an appropriate setting for their ceremony.

Cynthia and Carl's shared spiritual outlook contributed significantly to the shaping of their ceremony. Although she was raised Catholic and he Jewish, they embrace a nonsectarian philosophy based in part on close ties to nature and the environment. The mountaintop setting and their choice of an eclectic, female rabbi who incorporated their beliefs into the ceremony were crucial aspects of the wedding they envisioned.

The couple began actively planning their September wedding in March, giving them about six months. Because of Cynthia's grueling travel schedule, she had to make three or four major trips in the months prior to the wedding. So she and Carl decided to expand the planning team by asking her mother to help and hiring a wedding coordinator to take over some of the legwork. Seela, the wedding coordinator, had helped plan a wedding that had been an inspiration to both Carl and Cynthia.

Knowing that a professional was going to follow through with all the logistical details freed Cynthia and Carl to focus on what was most important to them: crafting a ceremony that reflected their beliefs and their spiritual connection (more on this later).

In Cynthia's absence, Carl got together with both Seela and Cynthia's mom, making decisions about everything from the buffet to decor. Fortunately, says Cynthia, bride and groom had similar ideas about what they wanted in terms of music, flowers, food, and such. So she felt confident that Carl would make the right choices.

And how did Carl feel about working with his future mother-in-law? "She's only about twelve years older than I am, so we're really more like peers," Carl explained. Trekking up to the mountain location several times to check things out gave them a unique opportunity to get to know each other. And although there were occasional disagreements, there was never the cliché son-in-law/mother-in-law struggle. They were a good team.

When Cynthia wasn't traveling, she and Carl attended to wedding arrangements collaboratively. Although the wedding coordinator followed through with many details, the couple conceived of everything themselves and made all the creative decisions—down to the color of the napkins and plates.

For example, they designed and came up with the wording for their invitations, spent days finding just the right kind of card stock, and worked closely with an artist friend of Cynthia's designing the graphics. To convey their spiritual message, the words "Please join us on the mountain in celebration of our marriage . . ." were printed over a delicate outline of Mt. Tamalpais.

Working out the logistics of having a wedding ceremony on top of a mountain and a reception in an adjacent forest grove took some doing. Because of the uncertainty of the weather, Cynthia and Carl had to arrange for a back-up location. The wedding invitations included specific instructions should it turn cold or rainy: vans would be available to take guests to a nearby community center. Consequently, the center had to be cleaned and ready for the event, should they need it. The contingency plan was this: by ten or eleven on the morning of the wedding, if the weather was bad, everything—flowers, tables, custom-made dance floor—would be transported to the alternate site. Seela was to execute this back-up plan, if necessary. Fortunately, the weather was beautiful.

The cost of renting the secluded oak grove, administered by the local Park Service, was about two hundred dollars. Although it was not possible to actually reserve the mountain-top, the Park Service knew Cynthia and Carl were having their wedding there and were kind enough to alert day-hikers. (Nevertheless, when the wedding party arrived on the day of the event, two nude sunbathers who had been dozing nearby had to discreetly move away, and hikers in the vicinity also made themselves scarce, respecting the ceremony taking place.)

There were a number of details to consider in conjunction with the mountain locale. Guests were given a list of things to be aware of on the mountain, including weather conditions and the need for comfortable clothing and shoes. (Two people actually arrived wearing hiking clothes!) Three friends had to be enlisted to carry a ninety-year-old uncle up the mountain on an "evacuation chair" festively decorated with colored balloons. Several others were assigned to transport both the table that was to be used as the ceremonial altar and chairs for older people and pregnant women. Again, Seela was there to see that all these specifics were attended to.

Other unwieldy but important props also needed to be shuttled to the site. Dancing was a definite priority, so a dance floor was constructed specifically for the wedding and temporarily installed in the forest knoll.

Carl, Cynthia, and Seela worked creatively with the caterer to cut down on the cost of the buffet. They had several conversations about saving X amount of money if one kind of salad was replaced with another, such as shrimp instead of lobster, and each such detail made a financial difference. The nouvelle cuisine was elegantly laid out in the forest grove. "Everything we did was in harmony with the environment," Cynthia assured us. "We used a natural tree stump to serve on and decorated that area with ferns and flowers."

But the portion of the wedding plans to which Carl and Cynthia devoted most of their energy was the ceremony itself. Every aspect, from the selection of an officiant, to their original "dialogue" and personally written vows, to the symbolic elements placed on the altar, was meticulously considered. And, as testimony to their shared spiritual beliefs, they were in sync on almost everything.

The choice of an officiant began with Cynthia's recollection of a female rabbi whom she had encountered at Princeton University as an undergraduate.

Even though I'm not Jewish, I feel culturally Jewish. I had seen this rabbi do a "moon ritual" at Princeton and was impressed with her at that time. Years later, I was at a wedding ceremony at the Ojai Foundation Center and I saw a write-up about her. I told Carl that if we ever got married, that's who I wanted. I wanted someone who was into Native American culture and respect for the earth. I didn't want a strictly religious ceremony, but one that would incorporate the things we believed in.

Carl had never met the rabbi but trusted Cynthia's judgment, adding:

I wanted a person who had a sense of humor, a good personality, warmth, and was nontraditional. It wasn't easy to find someone who would marry mixed couples. Religious people just kept saying no!

But the rabbi they wanted said yes. After speaking to her several times by phone, Cynthia and Carl knew they had found the ideal person to marry them.

Carl:
We didn't want an "authority figure." And she was someone who didn't have her ego attached to running the show. She was a guide and a facilitator, and very open to our needs.

The couple had to fly her in from New Mexico for the ceremony which meant paying for her round trip air fare, but they felt the extra expenditure was worthwhile, given their spiritual compatibility with her.

Then began the process of formulating the actual ceremony. Carl and Cynthia spent many brainstorming hours together. They checked out dozens of books on weddings—traditional, nontraditional, weddings in other countries—everything from serious psychological studies to practical how-to primers. "I wanted to get a full sense of this 'wedding thing,'" Carl explained.

As they got more information, they would call the rabbi who turned out to be as involved as they were! Carl recalled their conversations:

> *The rabbi would be on the phone with us throwing out ideas. I would tell her I had read something about having such and such in a ceremony, and she would say, "Actually, that's interesting because what I've done in certain ceremonies is thus and so." So she was right there with us, helping us devise what we wanted. We told her we wanted to build a chuppah but that it would be complicated getting it up the mountain. So she suggested we use a circle drawn in the earth instead. It's the same concept of creating a sacred space. We worked together. She never said, "I'm going to say this and this and this." We told her what we thought was important, and she listened.*

After their discussions with the rabbi, Cynthia and Carl crafted a ceremony essentially comprised of four parts: a "dialogue" between bride and groom, the vows, the ring ceremony, and blessings given by family and friends. Because they're both extremely committed to honest reflection and communication, and because they were determined to have their wedding mirror that integrity, we asked Cynthia and Carl to tell us how they went about writing such deeply felt material.

Cynthia:
> *It came together in a day or two, in a moment of divine inspiration. We meditated a lot on it. We also*

used some of the symbols described in On the Way to
the Wedding, *by Linda Schierse Leonard (New York: Dutton,
1992). I took a draft to Carl, and he edited and changed
some things. Then we did a back and forth over the
course of a day, and after that it was settled. If there
is such a thing as channeling, it felt like that was happening.*

Carl:
  *I was more responsible for drafting the ring
ceremony, because the vows came more fluidly to
Cynthia and the ring ceremony came easily to me.*

Cynthia:
  *I think it's very important to make it a dialogue.
We did this completely together. Wrote and talked
about everything together. It was really about staying
connected.*

In addition to Native American elements, Cynthia and Carl's
ceremony also included a number of Jewish traditions. They
both broke the glass (said to symbolize the fragility of life—
that even at a time of joy and celebration, there is suffering
elsewhere) and were later lifted up into the air seated in two
chairs while guests danced around them.

Then there were those aspects that were uniquely personal to
the bride and groom. The redwood burl altar was filled with
meaningful objects. There was a picture of Carl's late mother; an
earth-colored bowl filled with anointing oil, from Georgia, Russia (where Cynthia had traveled), which signified part of that
land; a white iris, their favorite flower; their wedding rock crystal; and a two-spouted Hopi wedding vase, which they and all
their guests drank from as a way of bringing everyone together.

Carl talked about his decision to have the photograph of his
mother on the altar:

*At our friends' wedding, they had an empty chair in memory
of those they would have wanted there but who had*

*died. I liked the idea, so I asked my dad to bring a
picture of my mother. It was a way of including her
in the ceremony, and it was also healing for my father
since he was very sad that my mom couldn't be at my
wedding.*

Although their overall planning experience sounds almost
too harmonious to be true, Cynthia and Carl did confess to instances of disagreement, frustration, and burnout. Carl remembered feeling "production anxiety" due to the enormity
of detail. "Plus I think I had some resentment over the fact
that two months prior to the event, Cindy took off for Russia
for six weeks. I felt that a lot of the burden had fallen on me."
Cynthia told her side of the story—what it was like coming
home from her Russian business trip, with only three weeks
left until the wedding.

*Almost everything had been arranged, but there was still
so much to do, and a lot of pressure. One day I was
so worked up about the logistics that I broke down
and told Carl, "Maybe I'm not ready for this." It wasn't
anxiety about getting married, it was doubt about getting
everything done in the way we wanted to. I was just
so overwhelmed. Well, Carl was incredible. He said,
"If it will make life easier for you to postpone or cancel
the wedding, that's fine with me." Once he said that, I
was able to relax, and we were able to get everything
done.*

Putting his resentment aside, Carl placed things in perspective by reminding himself—and Cynthia—that their relationship and well-being took precedence over even this wonderful
wedding they were planning. In reestablishing their sense of
priorities, they could both relax and take one day at a time.
The only other major conflict took place while they were
writing the "dialogue" portion of their ceremony. While the
vows and ring sections had been relatively effortless, Cynthia

had serious misgivings about the tone the dialogue was beginning to take.

> We had originally gotten the idea of the dialogue from
> a Buddhist wedding. It was really a "heart to heart"
> dialogue, a way of coming clean with one another.
> There's also a kind of Native American truth-telling aspect
> to it, feeling that when you talk to each other with a group
> of people witnessing it, that has a lot of power. So
> anyway, we had written this one draft that was very
> funny, parts even rhymed. But I felt very strongly that
> something was wrong. We had spent weeks on it, but
> it sounded too much like a script. Carl and I argued
> back and forth. Finally, we decided to throw it away
> and speak from our hearts.

On the day of the wedding, when it came time for the dialogue, Cynthia spoke spontaneously, "based on what I had jotted down in my mind." Since Carl didn't feel as comfortable extemporizing, he chose to read a letter he had written to Cynthia after a weekend they had spent together during their courtship. It very simply and poignantly communicated his growing love for her. Both were grateful that their prior argument convinced them to toss out the clever, scripted dialogue in favor of words that told their true story.

Cynthia and Carl's wedding was not only everything they hoped it would be, it was also a unique experience for those gathered on top of the mountain that day in September. The most memorable moment? "When ninety-year-old Uncle Irv got up and danced. No one expected him to, especially the people who had carted him up the mountain. He was inspired!"

Their efforts reveal that when a couple is spiritually and aesthetically on the same wavelength—and share equally in the conceptual and practical planning of their wedding—the results are nothing short of inspirational.

Tips from Cynthia and Carl

1. Do your homework. Go to the library and get books on traditional weddings so you know what to preserve and what to change in order to create an "in-the-moment" experience.

2. Look for inspiration from the weddings you've enjoyed attending.

3. Sit down at your computer and do your own planning lists—don't rely on the ones in books or magazines.

4. Develop a support system, whether it be mother-in-law, best friend, or wedding coordinator—so that you are free to focus on what is most important: your connection to your mate and being truly present at your own ceremony.

A Word About Wedding Consultants

"A wedding consultant is a surrogate mother, impartial listener, counselor, psychologist, best friend, and social secretary," says Vicki Giannone, certified wedding consultant with Creative Weddings in southern California. Basically, you're paying a wedding consultant to absorb the stress of planning a wedding so that you can have the fun of making creative decisions without the headache of working out every detail.

Because consultants plan dozens of weddings a year, they are familiar with which local vendors provide the best service for the best price. Negotiating on your behalf, they can save you hundreds of dollars and lots of running around. (As important as knowing which vendors to use is knowing which ones *not* to use!) Because florists, photographers, musicians, and caterers welcome the business generated by wedding consultants, they usually make a special effort to provide the consultant's clients with good service.

For couples who have busy work schedules and little free time, paying a wedding consultant to do the legwork is often worthwhile. And it doesn't mean you can't still call the shots. A good consultant will never try to "take over." They're there to facilitate, not dominate.

Some wedding consultants charge a percentage of the overall budget, whereas others charge a flat fee or an hourly rate. Vicki Giannone says she prefers a flat fee for a complete wedding planning service or an hourly fee for partial service. She believes a percentage can be unfair to both the client with a big budget and the consultant who works just as many hours on a small wedding as a larger one. (If a consultant does charge a percentage, make sure they're not steering you toward the most expensive vendors in an effort to increase their percentage.)

You should always have a contract with your wedding consultant, stipulating what their services will consist of and what their fee will be.

A good wedding consultant:

- Makes you feel comfortable
- Has experience in the business
- Stays within *your* budget
- Suggests ways to cut costs without sacrificing what you want
- Follows through in a reliable and timely fashion
- Reviews or prepares contracts with other wedding vendors
- Remains calm under stressful conditions ... but acts quickly and competently to resolve problems

The best way to maximize the services of a wedding consultant is to hire one very early in the planning stages.

A Collective Effort: Nancy and Matt

The Bride:	Age 39, second marriage
The Groom:	Age 35, first marriage
Ceremony:	Civil
Site:	Backyard
Guests:	75
Cost:	$3,000

Matt:

When I announced to my family that I was marrying Nancy, I could hear the whole clan breathe a collective sigh of relief. I think they thought I would never get married. My mom and dad, sisters, brothers, aunts, uncles, third cousins were absolutely thrilled, and everyone offered to help plan the wedding for us in my parents' backyard.

Nancy:

I was thrilled too. Because it was my second marriage, and I had been through the exhausting experience of doing it all yourself. I also knew what a fabulous party my in-laws were capable of throwing!

The mere thought of your entire extended family planning your wedding with you would be enough to make most brides and grooms flee to Las Vegas. Not Matt and Nancy. One of seven children, Matt is used to large groups of relatives. He says his family constantly jokes about not needing to call up friends to have a party.

My family is a party ready to happen. They're all real experienced in planning big events because we're always having family get-togethers of one sort or another. Even though we don't necessarily agree on

everything, we're pretty close knit. I was touched that
they all wanted to make our wedding a communal effort—
and it also felt natural.

Nancy was moved almost immediately by the warmth and
generosity of Matt's large family.

They all treated me like a daughter-in-law long before Matt
and I were engaged. And yet they also allow us our
independence. There was absolutely no stigma about
our decision not to have a church wedding, even though
my in-laws are devout Catholics. They respect who we
are as individuals but embrace us as part of the family.

Because Nancy's own parents are divorced and live in apart-
ments, it would have been impossible for either of them to
host the affair. And since this was her second wedding, she
was more than willing to give up some of the responsibility
this time around. She felt very comfortable with the idea of
Matt's family being co-planners.

Although money wasn't the main reason Nancy and Matt
decided on a "potluck wedding," it was a factor. Spending
more than three thousand dollars on their wedding would
have wiped out their savings, and it's difficult to host a catered
affair for seventy-five people without paying considerably
more than that. So their choice reflected both their desire to
make the wedding a family affair and their need to stay within
a limited budget.

Unlike the other two couples in this chapter, Matt and
Nancy had only two months in which to make the arrangements. How did they even begin to organize Matt's twelve siblings (including brothers-in-law and sisters-in-law), fifteen
aunts and uncles, two parents, and assorted nieces, nephews,
and cousins? Their first step was to initiate a planning
meeting, to which only Matt's immediate family and Nancy's
mom and sister were invited. Nancy described what went
down at the meeting:

*We broke things down and made lists, talking over who
would be good at what tasks, who had the time to
visit florists and call rental places, who had special
contacts, who was very dependable and who was sort
of dependable.*

And since Nancy and Matt both had tight work schedules
prior to the wedding, they assigned Matt's sister's place as
"Planning Central." All calls, questions, and input were
directed to her, and she kept them abreast. Again, Nancy:

*We were relieved to have the help, particularly since it
was a very hectic time for me at work. Also, I trusted
that Matt's family had good taste and would check
with us before making any major decisions. And one other
very important factor: since I had been to many of their
family gatherings, I knew firsthand that Matt comes
from a long line of incredible Italian cooks!*

Food was the least of their worries. One of Matt's sisters is
a gourmet chef with her own catering business, another is a
home-ec teacher who makes wedding and birthday cakes on
the side, and his mother and aunts all excel in the kitchen. At
the initial planning session, they decided to have a luncheon
buffet following the garden ceremony; Matt's mom and the
aunts would be responsible for about five or six Italian
entrées, a huge antipasto, and other assorted salads. The
home economics sister would make a three-tiered carrot cake
decorated with fresh flowers. And the gourmet sister would
cook and decorate a 12-pound poached salmon.

Some of the other tasks were assigned as follows:

- Selecting invitations: Matt and Nancy
- Addressing invitations: three teenage nieces
- Calling the local judge to perform the civil ceremony:
  Matt

- Arranging for rental of the tent for the backyard: Matt's father
- Arranging for rental of tables and chairs: Matt's middle brother
- Arranging for rental of china and flatware: Matt's mom
- Gardening (planting new flowers, getting the yard in shape): Matt's youngest brother
- Decorating the yard: Matt's mom and sisters
- Buying alcohol and drinks for the bar and hiring a bartender: Matt's brother-in-law
- Making party favors (tiny wrapped packages of candy almonds): Nancy's mom and sister

Since they were saving so much on food, Matt and Nancy decided to hire two people to oversee the buffet and wash dishes. They wanted everyone in the family to enjoy the actual wedding day and not be burdened with kitchen chores.

Nancy's mother offered to make arrangements with the florist, after consulting with Matt and Nancy as to their favorite styles and flowers. Again, some brides or grooms might have wanted more control, but Matt and Nancy were grateful to have someone else in charge. "I told my mom we wanted iris and lilies and other tropical flowers in contemporary arrangements, nothing too 'arranged' or formal looking. I had gone to this particular florist before, so I was confident we'd get what we wanted."

For the most part, plans went smoothly, each family member attending to his or her specific job, Matt and Nancy exercising veto power when necessary. There were, however, some rough times at "Planning Central." It seems the sister in charge there was embroiled in a kind of power play with another sister. They had a history of sibling rivalry and argued over everything from whether salmon really went with chicken cacciatore to whether or not to use a seven-year-old nephew's handmade silver bells as the bridal table centerpiece. Matt was caught in the middle.

One sister would call complaining about the other, and
there was no way I could take sides. I mean, here
they were both going out of their way for us—and
about to kill each other in the process!

Somehow it was easier for Nancy to step in during these
conflicts and cast the deciding vote. Her unbiased position in
the family and her role as the bride made it possible for the
sisters-in-law to accept salmon *and* chicken and nix the seven-
year-old's wedding bells.

I think they both meant well; they're just each very strong
personalities and used to being in charge. Even though
one was fielding all the calls and acting as the
wedding hot line, the other sister was equally involved
in organizing a lot of details. So there were those instances
when Matt would ask me to make some minor
decisions so that he wasn't stuck choosing between
one sister and the other.

When they opted for family participation in their wedding,
Nancy and Matt realized that they would have to accept certain elements not being exactly as they would have chosen.
Both felt that having the extra help and allowing everyone to
participate in their day was worth giving up a certain degree
of control—even if it meant wedding decorations that were a
tad tacky and unpredictable teenage DJs. Matt explained:

All in all, our wedding was perfect, and I treasure the memory
of it, I really do. But there were a few things . . . For
instance, Nancy and I probably would have chosen
fresh flowers to decorate the rented trellis, rather than the
artificial ones my mother and sister used. And then there
was the "Case of the Missing DJs." I had spent weeks
making up cassette tapes to play during the reception—
with all our favorite songs, as well as some Italian folk
songs I knew my family would get a kick out of. My brother

*had volunteered his two teenage sons to be the disc
jockeys, since they're both into music and sound
systems and stuff. Well, everything went fine for an hour
or so and then I realized there was no music and my nephews
weren't anywhere near the tape decks. I looked around
the yard and finally found them upstairs in my parents'
house chatting up a couple of very attractive distant
female cousins. It wasn't like it was a major catastrophe
or anything. And after all, they're just kids, not professionals.*

Matt and Nancy's willingness to roll with the punches made
their wedding that much more spontaneous. When the nephews were otherwise engaged, a musical brother-in-law decided
to fill in with an impromptu performance on his accordion—
which he just happened to have in the trunk of his car. "It was
actually the highlight of the wedding," Nancy remembers fondly.

*We didn't have a dance floor, but kids and uncles and
sisters got up and danced on the grass—and it was
great! There was no set program, just whatever Tony
decided to play. I have some wonderful photos of that
part of the reception.*

And speaking of photos, once again the couple's decision
was to use family rather than a professional, for reasons
Nancy explained:

*My sister is quasi-professional—she works for a local
magazine. We didn't want to spend a lot on a
photographer, so we told her we'd buy the film and
have her take mostly candids. We also asked her to shoot
some informal group shots of each branch of the family—
which on Matt's side was quite an undertaking.*

The results were satisfactory, but Matt and Nancy confess
that if they had it to do over, they might spring for a professional photographer. Matt told us why:

*For one thing, it was hard for her to enjoy herself and
be on duty taking photos. So there were some
moments she missed that we'll have to remember in
our mind's eye. Also, my parents' backyard has a lot of
trees, so the shadows were difficult to shoot around. A
professional photographer probably would have
known how to handle that a little better.*

In centuries past, cooperative weddings were the norm. An
entire community got together and hosted the event, spending
weeks preparing an elaborate feast and creating a festive atmosphere. Modern society has lost much of that spirit of cohesion.
But weddings like Nancy's and Matt's remind us of what we gain
when we're part of a group effort. Working together to bring
about something meaningful creates very special ties. Nancy
and Matt's sense of belonging to their families was strengthened
even more by sharing the wedding work with them.

Looking back on their day, Matt and Nancy insist that regardless of the glitches, theirs was the perfect wedding—made
even more memorable thanks to the efforts of those closest to
them. Family squabbles and artificial flowers aside, the event
was truly a labor of love.

Tips from Nancy and Matt

1. Before you begin delegating specific jobs to family or
    friends, think about who might be the best person for
    each task. Are they willing? Experienced? Reliable?

2. Give people the freedom to do the jobs they've offered
    to do, but keep control of major creative decisions—if
    they're very important to you.

3. Keep a sense of humor. Don't panic if your father-in-law
    chooses an orange tent for the backyard and it's your
    most detested color. Remember: it's only a tent.

4. If you'd prefer to receive money rather than gifts, tell a few close relatives, such as your parents and siblings. Then, when other relatives inquire as to what you and your mate want, those closest to you can spread the word.

5. Don't overwork your friends or family. Hire at least minimal professional help for the day of the wedding so guests can enjoy themselves.

6. Relax and enjoy the process. If your friends or family are helping out, it's not only about the results but the memories you'll have of working together to create something special.

CHAPTER 3

Priceless Weddings on Petite Budgets

"And your wedding bill comes to . . ."

invitations	$350
wedding rings	800
traditional wedding gown	2,000
tuxedo rental	100
officiant fee	150
tenting a large backyard	1,500
catered reception for 200 people @ $50 per person	10,000
rental of tables, chairs, china, silverware, and linens	1,300
photographer and photo package	1,500
videographer	500
wedding cake	500
flowers	1,500
5-piece band	1,000
personalized napkins and matches	50
favors	200
Total	**$21,450***

*Total does not include: marriage license, gifts for bridal party, hair stylist & makeup artist, liquor, honeymoon.

Traditional weddings are expensive. On the average, in fact, they cost about $16,000. If your yearly salary is $35,000, that's roughly 46 percent of your total earnings! Well aware of this, many couples take out loans or save judiciously for months, sometimes years, to pay for a wedding that fits the storybook image. Economic squeeze or no, they refuse to be deterred from enjoying the fairy-tale celebration they always envisioned. And if they can manage it, why shouldn't they do it up right? After all, a wedding is one of the most memorable events in a lifetime.

But other couples cannot afford to spend twenty thousand dollars or even ten thousand dollars no matter how long they save. Not only is most everyone's real income shrinking in these recessionary times, but creative couples often have additional financial pressures. Many are paying for their weddings solely on their own, with no assistance from parents. Others are already parents and must balance wedding finances with the needs of their children. Older brides and grooms may be thinking about their upcoming retirement or assisting aging parents. So there is a very real need to come up with alternatives to the conventional, expensive wedding.

Tight budgets don't mean, however, that beloved traditional touches cannot be retained and interwoven into a less costly event. With a little prioritizing, they can. Making lists of which aspects are most and least important to each of you will help you determine a realistic budget. For example, are stunning flower arrangements more or less important than a live band? Would you rather offer your guests an open bar and hors d'oeuvres or champagne and a sit-down lunch? Are you willing to relinquish a formal wedding gown to have your wedding at a beautiful site?

Or is formal even in your vocabulary? A number of couples told us they wouldn't have wanted a by-the-book wedding even if they could have afforded one. Relinquishing the pomp and circumstance not only saved them money, but freed them to be more creative. Necessity is the mother of invention, and invent they did . . . as you'll learn from the stories in this chapter.

But being unconventional isn't necessarily cheaper, and adhering to tradition isn't always expensive. The point is, having the kind of wedding you want is achievable regardless of your budget—if you know what you want. Before you even begin to juggle the figures, you need to consider just what you really wish your wedding to be. What extravagances are you unwilling to do without? Which would you be willing to sacrifice? What exactly do you want to get out of your day?

When we asked people that question, the responses we received were as unique as the personalities. "I wanted it to be really beautiful, a simple acknowledgment of spending my life with this person," said Alicia, a thirty-one-year-old bride who, together with her future husband, Michael, spent about one thousand dollars on their wedding. David, married twice before, said about his third marriage: "It was the first time I was going into something with my eyes open, and I wanted the wedding to be special, to mean something to us. It wasn't about other people, it was about the two of us." David and Charlotte's wedding cost five hundred dollars. And thirtysomething Maggie confessed that she wanted ". . . a celebration—a party without a time limit, with all my friends and family there to witness the event." She and her husband, Gerry, paid about five thousand dollars for their wedding. Although each of these couples learned their lessons about which corners should and shouldn't be cut, they all had the weddings they wished for . . . without breaking the bank. And so can you!

Tuxedo Barbecue: Alicia and Michael

The Bride: Age 31, first marriage

The Groom: Age 31, first marriage

Ceremony: Nondenominational

Site: Their home

Guests: 35

Cost: $1,000

Alicia:
*I'm very money-conscious; it's something that's
important to me. Shortly before our wedding, we
attended a friend's wedding where it was one hundred
dollars a plate, and her dress was five thousand dollars.
I just knew that wasn't for me, even if I had the money.*

Michael:
*Frankly, had we had all the money in the world, I would
have loved to have thrown a gigantic, catered bash. But
the way it turned out, it was very, very personal.*

Michael is a writer and Alicia a teacher and an actress. Like
many young couples in the formative stages of their respective
careers, they are struggling to balance modest incomes with
future plans and present necessities. The evening we met with
them in their small, rented house, Alicia's theater group was
rehearsing in the backyard—the same site where their wedding reception had taken place ten months earlier.

The couple had talked about marrying for months, but Michael's project deadlines had made it difficult to set the date.
Alicia's family lives three thousand miles away and couldn't
make the trip west for financial reasons, so her parents were
hosting a wedding reception for relatives on the East Coast.
The wedding date had to precede the already-planned family
reception, and yet time had somehow gotten away from the
newlyweds-to-be. Alicia explained:

*We kept postponing the wedding until we couldn't postpone
it any longer. My parents had planned their reception
for a certain day and we'd already bought the tickets
to fly back there, so when we woke up Saturday morning*

*two weeks before our trip, we looked at each other in
a panic and said, "We've gotta do it next weekend!!"*

Michael and Alicia settled on having the wedding at home;
they wanted a personal, nonreligious ceremony—and preferred to cut the guest list "down to the bone—only the people we felt closest to." Thirty close friends and Michael's
immediate family were invited. With such short notice, there
was no time to send out invitations; everyone was invited by
phone.

After spending a day or two contacting caterers and getting
prices, Alicia and Michael faced their first financial dilemma.
Although a friend in the catering business offered to give them
a break on the cost, they still couldn't swing it dollar-wise.
And asking their parents to contribute wasn't an option. "I
think my age had a lot to do with the fact that I didn't want
to ask my folks to pay for a wedding. I'd been out of the home
for years and supporting myself for so long," said Alicia. Michael concurred. "Being thirty-one rather than twenty-one affected my wanting to do it more independently."

So they put their creative heads together and came up with
a plan. They would host their own do-it-yourself wedding with
an outdoor barbecue following the evening ceremony in their
living room. Friends would cook up side dishes and salads;
Alicia and Michael would provide the meat and beverages, including wine, beer, and champagne. Another friend offered to
bake them a wedding cake.

Michael and Alicia's costs amounted to:

meat, sodas, alcohol	$150
folding chairs (30 @ $5 apiece)	$150
13 bouquets of flowers from the flower market	$60
100 candles	$25
Alicia's wedding ring	$325
Michael's wedding ring	$150
Alicia's dress and accessories	$120

Michael's red cummerbund and bow tie	$25
CD for the processional and recessional	$15
Total	$1,020

Because they wanted their ceremony to be intimate and reflective of their personal beliefs and values, the couple chose as their officiant someone close to both of them: Alicia's therapist, Marvin, who is also an ordained minister with the nondenominational Universal Life Church. The couple had alerted him in advance of their desire to have him officiate, placing him "on call" until they set the date. As soon as he received word, he came to the couple's home and helped them talk through what kind of ceremony they wanted. They all agreed that Marvin would greet the guests with a welcoming speech, after which the couple would toast themselves with champagne. Marvin would give his reflections on the theme of being separate individuals within a marriage union, followed by two poems read by friends. Michael and Alicia would read their vows to one another and exchange rings, and then another friend would play an original piece on the guitar. The ceremony would end with recorded recessional music by Purcell.

With just a few days remaining, the couple started writing their vows. Alicia said she found it difficult to concentrate with all the preparations to attend to. "If I could write mine over, I would," she stated apologetically. "I felt like what I wrote was too short and silly." Michael disagreed.

What Alicia wrote was great—simple and straightforward.
Mine, on the other hand, was long and involved. Being
a writer, I wanted to avoid anything that sounded too
contrived and have it be as much from the heart as possible.
So I spent a long time working on it, cutting out parts
and adding things—in an effort to be spontaneous!

While Michael was busy editing and re-editing his vows and choosing music for the processional (he bought and listened to about twenty classical CDs before choosing the Purcell piece), Alicia was out buying candles and flowers and chicken breasts.

Candlelight was an essential component of Alicia and Michael's wedding. Hoping to create an ethereal mood, they decided on a profusion of candles and a flickering fire in the fireplace that would serve as their living-room altar. The wedding was scheduled for five o'clock, but because it was November it was already dark at that hour. The path leading to their house would be lined with paper lantern–covered colored candles, and candles would be glowing everywhere indoors as well—lending a soft, magical quality to the whole house. "Friends told us later it was the same feeling as being in church."

In addition to thinking about food and decor, Alicia also had to buy her wedding dress that week. Knowing only that she wanted something long, she and a girlfriend headed for the local boutiques. They looked at a selection in many different colors and styles, but Alicia finally chose a long white lace dress—for only $70. "I wasn't necessarily thinking about looking like a bride, I just wanted something pretty. This dress was, and the price was right."

Michael's choice in wedding attire was also influenced by economics. He didn't want to go out and buy something if he could avoid it, and since he owned a nice tux, that made his decision easy. "It was either the tux or blue jeans. Actually, there are certain traditions I'm really not opposed to, and dressing up is one." His tux is navy blue and all he had to buy was a red cummerbund and red bow tie to go with it.

That premarital week wasn't all frantic shopping and nonstop work. Alicia's friends actually managed to pull off a surprise shower in the midst of everything else that was going on. They knew how busy Alicia was and that she probably wouldn't agree to one if they told her about it, so they cleverly schemed to get her to show up. A job interview was the only pretense they figured would work. Midweek Alicia received an audition call for a part in a children's play. When she arrived at the theater, someone pretended to be the director and others posed as actors waiting around for their appointments. After Alicia went through a complete audition as a giraffe, the entire theater began to applaud! Her friends had been hiding behind the curtain ready to surprise her, and she was completely fooled. The group then went back to a friend's apartment where they opened presents and played the videotape of the whole charade, à la "Candid Camera." Then they celebrated over lunch at a nearby restaurant.

Michael also told an amusing story about a friend wanting to throw him a bachelor party. Due to all the stress that week, he wasn't feeling up to a night on the town, but he agreed to have dinner at a sushi bar with a couple of close friends. Another buddy called to ask him what he wanted to do for his "official" bachelor party. Michael, who has no interest in that kind of thing, jokingly replied, "Why don't you just get a couple of bizarre women who'll agree to do anything . . ." The friend called back later and said, "Okay, I got a great place and found some women—I even bargained them down." Incredulous, Michael had to tell his gullible friend that his suggestion had only been a joke!

The wedding day approached with most elements in place, but Michael and Alicia were both feeling pretty stressed out. From the moment they decided to put the wedding together on such short notice, Michael was doubtful they could pull it off.

The pressure of having so little time was a great source of tension, and it made me become very negative.
I remember complaining the night before the wedding, saying the candles were going to set the curtains on fire and the barbecue was gonna be tacky and people were going to get barbecue sauce all over their nice clothes and stuff.

Alicia remembers the grumpiness too. She said she was cleaning and vacuuming during Michael's tirade, and when she asked him to check on the marinade, a fight ensued. At the heart of it, was Michael's resentment over having too much to do at his own wedding.

Michael:
*Here we were cleaning and cooking—I was
worrying about having enough bowls for marinating
the chicken—and it just didn't feel like what was supposed
to happen before your wedding! I guess I wanted somebody
else to be taking care of everything at that point.*

Michael acknowledged that Alicia was very tolerant of his moodiness that night, adding that they both experienced a "roller coaster of emotions" that entire week. Not only were they doing almost everything themselves in an effort to cut costs, they only had a week in which to do it all! Both of them conceded that were they to do it over, they would ask more friends to help out.

So how did their big day turn out? The house was aglow, transformed by candlelight and the shimmering fire. The fireplace altar welcomed bride, groom, and officiant as they stood before their closest friends who were gathered in the intimacy of the couple's living room. The ceremony went fairly smoothly—aside from some technical difficulties with the CD player at the beginning of the processional. Marvin's words were in keeping with the themes agreed upon beforehand—although, Michael recalled, there were a few surprises.

*Marvin referred to marriage as a "love-sex relationship,"
and we didn't know he was going to say that—but
I appreciated the thought. It was nice because it was
very down to earth—you don't hear that too often at
weddings!*

You also don't hear raunchy blues guitar too often at weddings, but the ceremony culminated with a friend's original blues guitar piece, a "show-stopper," as Michael put it. All in all, it was a celebration personally tailored to Alicia and Michael's tastes and feelings. "The ceremony was one big giant great moment," said Michael. "From the minute we stepped into the living room that night, I was in another world." Alicia was also overcome with emotion, confessing that though she tried very hard not to, she cried at her own wedding.

The guests loved the barbecue reception, the closeness of their small group of friends, and the casual air of the whole celebration. Most stayed well into the evening, enjoying the down-home food and conversation. Unlike bridal couples at larger events, Michael and Alicia were able to spend time with each of their guests.

Unfortunately, Alicia became overly concerned with being a good hostess. Although two friends were tending the barbecue, and others offered to help during the course of the evening, Alicia found herself picking up plates and constantly making the rounds cleaning up. "I was a waitress for eleven years, and it was hard for me to sit back and have a good time, even at my own wedding." She realized too late that prior to the wedding she should have assigned a few friends to clean up during the reception.

Michael also became exhausted that evening, a delayed reaction to the week's frantic pace. Putting his own well-being ahead of social convention, he came up with a logical solution. He simply slipped into the bedroom, locked the door, and took a nap for about an hour! When he reemerged, he rejoined the festivities much refreshed.

By midnight, most of the guests had departed, leaving only a core of close friends who stayed until 2:00 A.M. talking and having a great time.

Michael:
One of the nicest things about our wedding was that at the end of the evening, it stopped being this big overwhelming thing and was just what we wanted—an intimate circle of friends.

Both he and Alicia felt that the personal quality and simplicity of their wedding made it special. They didn't have to concern themselves with the compulsory agenda of larger, more formal weddings—most of which has no relevance to them. Although they could have done without the pressure of planning the entire event in a week, and though they now understand the importance of asking friends to help, they're happy with the kind of wedding they had. Michael explained why:

We spent practically no money, and it was just as terrific. Money is not what determines the quality of your wedding. If there are the right feelings involved, it will be wonderful.

Tips from Alicia and Michael

1. Don't try to do everything yourself—even if you're having a small wedding at home. Ask willing friends to help, and discuss who will be doing what before the reception gets underway. Or . . . consider paying for one or two people to serve and clean up the day of the wedding. (Neighborhood teenagers might do it for less.)

2. Tell friends on a tight budget that their help with the wedding should be considered their wedding gift to you.

3. Don't forget to check out your local wholesale flower market. You can save a lot of money and get the freshest flowers.

4. If you're having friends take photographs for you, be sure they have a good 35mm camera and know how to use it—and buy lots of extra film.

5. Appreciate the uniqueness of a do-it-yourself/potluck wedding. The peach-colored, almond-flavored wedding

cake our friend made for us looked like an adobe building ... but it tasted better than any wedding cake we could have bought!

6. Above all, try to relax and enjoy your wedding ... even if it means letting the dishes pile up!

Our Secret Garden: Charlotte and David

The Bride:	Age 50, third marriage
The Groom:	Age 52, third marriage; son, age 27, from previous marriage
Ceremony:	Civil
Site:	Hotel
Guests:	23
Cost:	$500

Charlotte:
We wanted to avoid a lot of expense and a lot of preplanning—all that stuff you go through with rehearsals and dinners, who wears what and who stands where.

David:
We were driving back after a weeklong trip together in December, and it was pouring rain all down the coast. It was just gorgeous. We were talking about where to have the wedding and all of a sudden I remembered this wonderful old hotel in the town where we'd gone to college together. Because we had met there, the place had a lot of meaning for us.

More than twenty-five years ago, David and Charlotte both got married for the first time and attended each other's weddings. In fact, Charlotte was the maid of honor at David's wedding and David's ex-wife was one of Charlotte's five bridesmaids. Charlotte, David, and David's ex-wife attended college together and were then—and still are—close friends. Both first weddings were huge, traditional affairs—formal attire, receiving lines, bridesmaids, the whole nine yards. Although Charlotte and David have some happy memories of their respective events, both agreed that there had been "way too many people" and that the experience had been unbearably taxing and stressful. "It was this blur of trying to greet everybody and not really enjoying the moment. Afterward, I didn't even remember what went on," Charlotte recalled.

This time around, the couple was clear about putting the focus where it belonged: on the two of them. They didn't want to spend a lot of money, but they did think it would be wonderful to be married in a beautiful setting in the town where they'd met so long ago. After all, their relationship had quite a history. They'd been good friends when they were young, kept in contact for many years, went their separate ways, and then rediscovered each other after having come through some rough times.

The rainy-afternoon car trip David described was the last day of a gloriously romantic "premarital honeymoon." The two had spent the weekend celebrating alone what they would soon make official in the company of an intimate group of friends. Deliriously happy together even after spending the last eight hours on a rain-soaked highway, the couple impulsively decided to drive another half hour to the town where they'd first laid eyes on each other.

The minute they saw the hotel, they made their decision. They loved the elegant, century-old architecture and were especially drawn to "the most beautiful sunken rose garden with a little bridge going over it." Renovated since their college days, this was now a first-class establishment: marble floors, Persian rugs, exotic flower arrangements filling the sweeping foyers, and a maze of alluring walkways threading the immaculately tended botanical gardens.

The problem was that the cost of renting the garden for a wedding ceremony, even a small one, would have been almost $500—much more than their modest incomes could afford for the site alone. So they came up with a daring idea. They would check into the hotel on the Saturday night before the wedding (for the special weekend rate of only $119 a night), tell their twenty-some guests to meet them in the lobby Sunday morning, at which time they would all casually stroll out to the garden and discreetly witness the marriage of David and Charlotte. Then, instead of a full-blown reception, the group would partake of the Sunday brunch that the hotel routinely offers, and at three o'clock make their way to the hotel's Sunday "tea dance" featuring a jazz-swing combo, also a regularly scheduled event.

Once they set the date—January 19, only a month after they visited the hotel—Charlotte and David quickly agreed on who to invite. The private room where they would have brunch could only accommodate twenty-five people, so that dictated their absolute guest limit: twenty-three. Only their "very, very closest friends," as well as a few family members, were invited, including David's twenty-seven-year-old son, who would be best man, and Charlotte's niece, who would serve as maid of honor. One other stipulation concerning their twenty-three guests: they would have to pay for their own thirty-five-dollar-per-person brunch. "We knew we couldn't afford to treat everybody, and our friends understood that perfectly," said Charlotte. The couple specified "No wedding gifts." Each friend's presence at the brunch was considered their gift to the newlyweds.

Charlotte and David would host a backyard marriage celebration party a few months later for those friends and family not invited to the wedding. Because everyone understood the couple's limitations and intentions, no one was offended. "I didn't want to get into that whole thing of worrying about other people's feelings," David remarked. "Besides, everyone knew this was something we were doing for ourselves, so there were no hurt feelings."

Wanting to keep the ceremony short and simple but reflective of the deep love they felt for each other, David and Charlotte asked an old college friend, now a Superior Court judge, to officiate. Actually, the judge insisted! "If I don't perform the ceremony," she lovingly threatened, "I'll never speak to you again!" Charlotte and David were delighted. With so much shared history, the couple trusted her to write their ceremony. "She's known us both for thirty years, through a lot of ups and downs. So she appreciated how happy we were and was very happy for us."

Since the "reception" would consist of the hotel brunch and tea dance, there was little else to arrange in terms of decor or other amenities; the hotel was always beautifully and festively appointed. A girlfriend offered to make Charlotte's bouquet, a nosegay of baby peach-colored roses, and Charlotte ordered a heart-shaped spice cake, which her niece agreed to pick up and bring with her to the hotel the day of the wedding. David's son and the judge's husband would bring their cameras and take snapshots.

Everything was in place, except for Charlotte's dress. Wanting her entire wedding experience to be relaxed and stress-free, she promised herself she wouldn't fret over what to wear. But after a long day of shopping, she came home and told David she couldn't find anything suitable for the wedding. She had, however, bought a terrific dress to wear on job interviews. David asked her to try it on for him. "That's it! Wear it! It's the perfect dress for the wedding!" he said as soon as he saw her. Simple but beautiful, it was a long-sleeved gray flannel dress with an elegant fitted top, belted waist, and full skirt. Charlotte was extremely relieved that she didn't have to look like "the clichéd bride." Blushing as she told us this story, she turned to David and asked tentatively, "But I still looked like a bride, didn't I?" He smiled and nodded. What had made Charlotte look like a bride, he revealed, was "her glow."

Even when a couple insists they want to be rid of all the

tired old wedding customs, some conventions are dearly beloved. Charlotte kept the "something borrowed, something
blue . . ." tradition alive. She borrowed her mother's old set of
pearls, which now belonged to her niece. Because her mother
is deceased, Charlotte wanted to wear the pearls as a way of
feeling her mom's presence at the wedding. She bought herself a blue garter, and her new dress completed the sentimental prescription.

David didn't buy a new suit but wore a beautiful black
Italian one he already owned and a tie that is Charlotte's favorite. He did, however, purchase black silk pajamas for the prenuptial night!

The day before the wedding, the newlyweds-to-be checked
into the hotel, had a massage before dinner, and luxuriated in
their posh surroundings. After an early morning walk, they ate
breakfast by the pool and then went upstairs to get ready for
their wedding. "That's when I cried for an hour," Charlotte con-
fided.

*I went completely to pieces. David had gotten dressed and
looked so handsome, and I just felt like I wasn't going
to be able to come up to it. Like I was gonna be old and
ugly and fat. That's what I felt—all of a sudden.*

Apparently, hormones and wedding-day tension conspired
to put Charlotte on edge. But after she showered, fixed her
hair, applied her makeup, and got dressed, she felt much
more relaxed.

*I looked at myself in the mirror and said, "Not bad." And
when I walked down to the lobby and saw David, he
had so much love pouring out of him that I felt like the
most beautiful woman in the whole world.*

The "secret" wedding went off without a hitch. In a secluded part of the rose garden, the group of twenty-three
friends encircled David and Charlotte to witness their vows.

The judge quickly performed the ceremony, pictures were taken, and afterward the couple not only kissed each other but everyone in attendance. Charlotte and David laughingly recall a few passersby who came strolling by during the ceremony and, not knowing what was going on, stopped to observe; the curious strangers appear in several of the cherished wedding snapshots.

The luxurious private room where they had their brunch was fit for royalty. Yet Charlotte, David, and their guests were enjoying its regal intimacy at a nominal per person cost. Friends made speeches, everyone raved about the sumptuous feast, and Charlotte tossed her bouquet into the "crowd" of three single women. Then they all proceeded to the tea dance where valentine-shaped spice cake and a spicy swing combo awaited them. They danced, they nibbled, they sipped—in celebratory splendor. And apart from a few other hotel guests, the wedding party essentially had the room to themselves.

Drawing on the wisdom that comes with age and the romanticism that envelops lovers of every age, Charlotte and David crafted a wedding that eliminated the hoopla but not the elegance. For the price of a night in a hotel, a heart-shaped cake, a gray flannel dress, and a pair of black silk pajamas, they had the most romantically elegant wedding they could ever have wished for.

Tips from Charlotte and David

1. Do what you want to do; don't cave in to other people's expectations and fantasies about who you are.

2. If you've decided a small, intimate wedding is what you want, do it. Don't worry that you'll hurt everyone's feelings by not inviting them. You can throw a bigger, more casual party later . . . your real friends will understand.

3. If you're older and/or have already outfitted a kitchen and household, consider an alternative to traditional wedding gifts. We asked friends who attended our backyard wedding party to bring food for the homeless instead of a wedding present.

4. A beautiful setting for your wedding need not cost a fortune. Even if you don't feel comfortable "bootlegging" a hotel wedding as we did, there are other creative solutions: parks, public gardens, beaches, and such.

5. When keeping costs down is imperative, close friends will understand the need to throw a "no-host" reception, especially if you tell them their participation will serve as their wedding gift to you.

Bed and Breakfast Vows: Maggie and Gerry

The Bride:	Age "thirtysomething," first marriage
The Groom:	Age "thirtysomething," first marriage
Ceremony:	Protestant
Site:	Bed and Breakfast inn
Guests:	80
Cost:	$5,000

Gerry:
Whatever she wanted, I wanted her to have. But at our age you understand money more and you don't want to waste a bunch of it.

Maggie:
We wanted it to be a great party and didn't feel comfortable having it in a restaurant or a hotel,

*because you're limited to only so many hours. You also
can't bring your own liquor or they charge you to open
it. So we found a way to avoid the expense of all that.*

In Maggie and Gerry's case, finding the right *place* for their
ceremony and reception was the key to having the wedding
they wanted at a price they could afford. There were a
number of considerations. First, they wanted a certain degree
of formality in their ceremony. Maggie insisted on a minister
who would begin with the line "Dearly beloved, we are gathered here today . . . " But they didn't want a church wedding
because they don't consider themselves that religious and felt
it would be hypocritical. Second, although they liked the idea
of having the ceremony and reception in the same place, they
couldn't afford to rent a hotel or restaurant for the length of
time they wanted the reception to last—indefinitely. Also, they
had to think about how to accommodate out-of-town family
because local hotels are very expensive.

While leafing through a magazine, Maggie hit on a clever
idea that seemed to satisfy all their requirements. In the magazine's index she found a list of local Bed and Breakfast establishments, and decided that one of these small hostelries
would be the ideal site. She and Gerry visited quite a few of
them, but many had restrictions about bringing in food, liquor, or music. Others were too costly. They finally settled on
a charming little Cape Cod-style inn near the beach, which offered to rent them all nine guest rooms as well as the "living
room" and garden courtyard for only $1,700. They would es-
sentially have the run of the entire place for twenty-four hours.
More like a home than a hotel, it was beautifully appointed
and had a lovely seaside view.

Next, the couple set to work planning the menu. They were
keen on having a nighttime affair, so they scheduled the ceremony for five o'clock. This meant cocktail-party food would
be appropriate—and less expensive than a buffet dinner. But
because they wanted the party to last into the night, the fare
had to be substantial and plentiful enough to take the place

of dinner. They couldn't afford to pay a caterer, so they researched various take-out places in the area, sampling food as they went. Finger sandwiches were ordered from the supermarket deli, and Maggie would pick up premade hors d'oeuvres from a discount food and party supply house. And the pièce de résistance: fresh jumbo shrimp, lots of it. "We must have spent three hundred dollars on shrimp—but it was delicious and impressive!" Maggie's feeling was that no matter what else was being served, she wanted one very classy delicacy. And because they were saving money by buying the food themselves, they could afford to splurge on one such item.

As for liquor, they decided on a full bar, again realizing a tremendous savings by purchasing it themselves at local discount stores. A bartender and two hostesses were hired for the evening at a total cost of $250. The hostesses would oversee the food, most of which was cold and required minimal preparation. The Bed and Breakfast relaxed their rules and gave the couple access to the small kitchen when necessary. Tables and chairs, china and glasses had to be rented.

Although cutting the guest list is an obvious cost-saver, Maggie and Gerry didn't want to economize in that way. Maggie especially wanted everyone she knew and loved to be there. They had three groups of people to invite: family, friends, and a number of fellow musicians from Maggie's days as a punk singer. No one was excluded, and the guest list came to about 80 people, roughly maximum capacity of the inn's courtyard.

Maggie designed their invitations to be both traditional and creative by decorating the edges of the high-grade white rag paper with glitter. She also used a lacy opaque overlay. The wording denoted that the bride and groom were hosts of their own celebration: "We cordially request the pleasure of your company at our wedding . . ."

Only one problem arose with respect to the guest list: children. Because it was a cocktail party that they hoped would continue late into the night, the couple preferred an adults-only affair. When friends and family called to ask if they could bring their kids, the couple informed them of their preference. But because Gerry's folks felt uncomfortable about prohibiting children in the family from coming, it turned out there were a half dozen young ones at the wedding. Although they didn't disrupt the festivities in any way, Maggie was upset about the apparent double standard applied to the "no kids" rule. Worse, she was annoyed with herself for getting so upset and fretting over relatively minor details.

> *I got it in my mind that everything should be perfect. But why should a wedding be perfect? Nothing else is! It's just that emotionally things get out of hand and you end up dumping it on your family.*

In the course of planning her wedding Maggie became a perfectionist when she never had been one before. In fact, Gerry was shocked at the emotional transition. Maggie had always been "laid back" and not the least bit compulsive. "I had never seen her like that before!" And Maggie had never felt like that before either. "I cried a lot," she told us.

Our culture invests your wedding day with such exalted significance it's not surprising that brides and grooms are overwhelmed by the pressure to make every detail perfect. But as with Michael and Alicia, a large part of Maggie's prewedding-day stress was caused by taking on too much of the work herself and not planning for enough outside help. The day before the wedding she was running around picking up hors d'oeuvres, shopping for flowers to decorate the courtyard, and having a final fitting on the custom-made beaded bustier wedding dress a friend was making for her. Rather than offering to pitch in with last-minute chores, as Maggie assumed they would, her mother and sister (both from out of town) wanted the frazzled bride to take them sightseeing! "They thought they were on vacation and kind of forgot I was having a wedding! I was like pulling my hair out thinking, 'Help me!' "

She was thinking "Help me!" but wasn't actually saying anything. Unless a friend or family member insisted on taking on a particular task, Maggie didn't ask.

> *I wasn't organized or assertive enough to make up a list of what needed to be done and tell people to do it. When someone offered to help, it was hard for me to say, "Oh, yeah, at three o'clock go pick up the cake . . ."*

Of course Gerry did his share—recorded hours of music tapes, bought the alcohol, strung lights in the courtyard, helped get the food trays ready, set up the flowers on all the tables, and generally "directed traffic." But, as Maggie lamented, "we didn't have a mother figure to take charge." Given that Maggie and Gerry were on a tight budget, what might they have done to prevent the feeling of being overwhelmed by so many last-minute details?

- Had they been willing to cut costs somewhere else, they could have hired a professional wedding coordinator, an organizational "mother figure." (Although some are men.) *Cost:* About forty dollars per hour.
- Or, they could have assigned one friend or family member to take charge of overseeing all details the day before and the day of the wedding. *Cost:* Only the assertiveness necessary to ask a favor.

Even though they had to cope with the rigors of doing everything themselves, Maggie and Gerry managed to put the stress behind them once the wedding got underway. A singer friend began the celebration by dedicating "Stand By Me" to the bridal couple before their short, simple ceremony. Maggie looked stunning in her very original (and finally completed!) beaded creation; Gerry felt great in his hip new pin-striped jacket. Guests were enthralled with the charming location and impressed with the lavish hors d'oeuvres (who would have guessed supermarket sandwiches??). No longer feeling "wigged out," Maggie and Gerry had a great time at their own wedding, a high point being the lighting of their wedding cake with Fourth of July sparklers!

The event was just the kind of party they had hoped for—informal, relaxed, and long-lived. In fact, it was such a success, bride and groom finally had to kick everyone out at 1:00 A.M.!

Tips from Maggie and Gerry

1. When selecting a site, research the lesser-known inns and bed and breakfasts in your area. The ambience is more romantic and they may be able to give you a better deal than the average hotel or restaurant.

2. Consider finger foods as an alternative to dinner—but make them substantial and abundant.

3. Buy your own liquor, if possible. You'll realize a tremendous savings.

4. Spend as much as you can on service personnel the day of the wedding. They're worth it!!

5. When people ask if you need any help, say yes . . . and then be specific.

6. It's better (and less expensive) to have great performers on tape than a second-rate band live.

7. Whether you're coming up with a budget or coming down with a major case of wedding frenzy, keep in mind that your wedding is only a party; your marriage is going to last a lifetime.

Twenty-two Tips for Petite Budgets

1. The most obvious way to cut costs is to cut your guest list. Think about the people who really matter to you and try to avoid inviting too many others out of sheer obligation.

2. Prices vary significantly depending on region of the country; if your wedding is in Sioux City rather than New York City, you'll realize a tremendous savings. Everything costs more in large urban areas.

3. If you choose a reasonably priced paper stock, simple, traditional invitations are actually less expensive than those with creative flourishes (unless, like Maggie, you add the creativity yourself).

4. Thermographed invitations will cost you less than engraved ones ... and you can't really tell the difference unless you turn the invitation over to check for indentations!

5. Save yourself extra printing costs and half the postage by putting "RSVP" on the invitation, rather than enclosing a reply card.

6. You'll save money on sites, caterers, florists, and musicians by marrying in a less popular "wedding month." June, of course, is the most popular; other months vary according to region of the country. Similarly, you'll probably pay less if you marry on a Friday or Sunday rather than a Saturday.

7. Check with your Chamber of Commerce and Parks Department for information on civic buildings, historic mansions, and other public sites. They provide a more interesting—and more reasonable—wedding location.

8. A morning or early afternoon wedding will reduce costs, because brunch and lunch are less expensive than dinner.

9. If you're having an early evening wedding, a cocktail party is a less costly alternative to dinner.

10. Having waiters pass around hors d'oeuvres is more economical than a buffet because you have more control over how much is served.

11. If the caterer is charging a per person fee, have someone in your bridal party call guests to confirm who's coming. (One couple told us twenty-five people who RSVP'd that they would attend didn't show up!)

12. Serve champagne and wine instead of having an open bar.

13. Hire a DJ rather than a live band—or, cheaper still, make your own tapes. (Just be sure to arrange for good sound equipment.)

14. Choose flowers that are regional and in season.

15. After a church ceremony, have the ceremonial floral arrangements brought to the reception site where they'll perform double duty.

16. Select a top-notch photographer, but opt for a less costly "package" of photos.

17. Have your guests be the photographers. Buy five or ten disposable cameras and let them take the candids. (Be sure to have someone collect the cameras when the party's over.)

18. If you're married to the idea of an elaborate wedding gown, consider renting one. Bridal rental shops offer an excellent selection and tremendous savings.

19. Search out a talented seamstress who, for much less, can create the same dress you saw in a bridal salon.

20. Consider buying a simpler dress that makes you feel just as beautiful and bridal but doesn't come from a

bridal department or salon. You'll walk down the aisle richer.

21.   Save the one hundred an hour charged by limousine companies by asking your brother, uncle, or best friend to drive you in their spruced-up Chrysler or Toyota. Insist on sitting in the backseat while they play chauffeur-for-a-day.

22.   Take advantage of your friends and family. Consider how their talents and expertise might be used to replace the many costly vendors whose pockets you'll be lining. You'll not only save money, you'll also create a more heartfelt experience.

CHAPTER 4

Ceremonial Fusion: Intercultural and Interfaith Weddings

Let me not to the marriage of true minds
Admit impediments.   —Shakespeare,
                          Sonnet CXVI

We live in a pluralistic society, a vibrant jumble of peoples with diverse beliefs, ethnicities, races, and faiths. Multiculturalism is our foundation; we have always been and will continue to be a people bound by our diversity. As the social stigma of "marrying outside of one's kind" continues to diminish, individuals of disparate backgrounds have unlimited opportunities to meet, fall in love, and wed one another. Statistics show that intermarriage of all sorts has been on the rise since the 1960s.

But, then, why should this surprise us? Love transcends color, religion, and ethnicity. Love dissolves the barriers that divide us. Love unites.

Intercultural and interfaith couples know that if they want a wedding that mirrors their distinctive backgrounds, mainstream wedding planners can take them just so far. Etiquette is designed to reduce wedding ritual to a predictable formula, and the richness of diversity is often sacrificed for the comfort of conformity.

As a result, couples whose differences matter as much as their similarities must reinvent ritual or risk having a wedding that is less than the sum of their distinctive parts. Each of the couples you will meet in this chapter have recalculated the symbolic elements of their wedding ceremonies to embody their divergent cultural backgrounds or religious beliefs.

Padmini and Michael, an intercultural couple, planned back-to-back ceremonies, one civil and one Sri Lankan, that preserved the integrity of their separate identities. Lynnette and Akil, an African-American couple, transformed Western nuptials into an eclectic Pan-African wedding using customs and accents from Nigeria, Ethiopia, Egypt, and Lesotho. And, Leslie and Mark, an interfaith couple, balanced Christian and Jewish components into one co-officiated ceremony.

Their weddings will serve as a sampling of the countless alternatives that can be exquisitely conceived and truly inspiring. Tailoring your wedding to preserve and combine your respective traditions, is a unique opportunity to make a powerful statement about how you define your own identity and what you believe is at your very core. Moreover, a ceremony that celebrates your cultural or religious heritage can enhance your understanding of who you both are as husband and wife.

Saris and Champagne:
Padmini and Michael

The Bride:	Age 26, second marriage
The Groom:	Age 35, first marriage
Ceremony:	Civil/Sri Lankan
Site:	Historic house
Guests:	150
Cost:	$12,000

Love has never let national borders or ethnic differences stand in its way. And neither did Padmini and Michael, who married two years ago in a dual ceremony that both honored and transcended their respective multicultural roots. What mattered more than their diverse origins and upbringing was their shared philosophy of life: a preference for simplicity and an emphasis on honesty. By embracing their differences and similarities, Padmini and Michael were able to weave together a wedding that was a cloak of many colors.

Their lives began nine years apart, almost to the day, on distant continents that are worlds apart in every imaginable way. American-born Michael, part Irish, part Polish, spent his formative years in a "mixed-neighborhood" in Buffalo, New York. Padmini, whose mother is Sri Lankan and whose father is "a proper English gentleman," was born in northern India but was raised successively in Pakistan, Bangladesh, Malaysia, and Singapore. Growing up, Padmini was always going back and forth to visit her English grandmother in Devon, England, the country she considered her home base until she moved to the United States to attend college.

Michael has never had any difficulty accommodating his own ethnic mix. And as far as Padmini's is concerned, he has never once thought of his wife as a "woman of color." To Michael, the Sri Lankan part of her represents one point on the continuum of her identity, not a difference that separates them in any way.

But Padmini found that reconciling her own mixed origins wasn't always as effortless. The reactions she receives from others continually force her to define herself.

*I am this person and that person. When people ask me
where I am from I say, "I am half English and half
Sri Lankan." Then they look at my skin color, my eyes,
and my hair and say, "Oh, you're Sri Lankan. How exotic!"
When I am alone, I tend to be more British, even though
I do make the occasional curry. But then, when I am
with my mother's family, the Sri Lankan side pops out.*

The style of Padmini's first wedding and her feelings about it reflect this split in her identity. The nuptials took place in a Catholic church. It was a huge fairy-tale affair, "by the book" to be exact. A part of her believed that by having an enchanted wedding, she might also have an enchanted future. But, by the end of the day, Padmini had the vague sense that she'd done something for everyone else except herself. When her marriage ended less than a year later, she realized her picture-perfect wedding had had little to do with a real marriage. She promised herself that if and when she wed again, it would be completely different.

This lesson was invaluable. By the time she met Michael and married him a little more than a year later, her expectations were more grounded and her personal identity more clearly defined. Finally, Padmini was ready to plan a wedding for herself, one that symbolized not only union with her lover, but also her own authentic self. She had arrived at a point in her life where she wanted to express who she is. "I truly feel that I am a mix and have deep feelings for both," Padmini stated in her lovely English accent, "On my wedding day I wanted to show every side of myself."

Around the same time Michael, too, had reached a new understanding of himself. A bachelor until age thirty-five, he finally felt mature enough to marry for the first time. For years Michael's family had wondered if he would ever settle down. They looked forward to meeting their new daughter-in-law-to-be with reserved anticipation and curiosity. But, given the geographical distance between them, that meeting didn't occur until the night before the wedding. Michael wanted the wedding to be a kind of "kickstart to our life," one that would showcase their love and put to rest anyone's lingering doubts that theirs would be a good marriage.

Part of what was behind the wedding was for people to see what Padmini and I are all about. I wanted it to be for us but also to address some of the family issues. The fact that Padmini had been married before

and then divorced created a major wave in her family.
Naturally, there were questions in their mind.

Then there was my family who had been waiting
for me to get married for a long time. My family, with
the exception of my mother, are hip people. Hip meaning
there are no racial attitudes. But they were wondering,
too. So the wedding was a way for Padmini to
introduce herself to my family and my friends. We both
knew that the first impression was important.

Although Padmini and Michael are both Catholics, neither is devout and neither wanted a church ceremony, even if they could have had one. Instead, they chose to take their vows at an historic hacienda-style house set high on the bluffs overlooking the Pacific Ocean. The site conveniently provided the catering and food service, but, unfortunately, Sri Lankan cuisine was out of the question.

Deciding on the guest list came next. It was here that the couple had to abandon their initial vision of "a small buffet for 50" as the pressure of family politics mounted. The number of invitees soon swelled to 200. Michael tensely agreed to revise the plan in deference to Padmini's mother's concern that no one in her large, extended family be excluded. In the end, Padmini's side of the guest list outnumbered Michael's about three to one. The guest list was "trimmed" to 150.

Almost immediately, their original budget of $6,500 ballooned to $12,000. Since Padmini and Michael had intended to pay for the wedding themselves, with Michael assuming the lion's share, it was clear something had to be done. Padmini was faced with a dilemma. On the one hand, the wedding, as planned, was quickly draining their bank account. On the other, the bride didn't want to ask for help, because her family had already paid for her first wedding. Padmini's mother refused to make concessions. Finally, she reluctantly took the issue to her father.

I told him that all we wanted and could afford was a small wedding. Now that the guest list was 150, we couldn't afford it. He came back to me and without me initiating it said, "I'm your father and I would love to make a contribution."

The couple cut costs where they could. They provided the liquor to the site. The bagpiper, who Michael thought would lend a touch of Great Britain to the celebration, went by the wayside. Padmini's mother bought flowers at the local flower mart, knowing the service staff at the site would do the table arrangements.

But there were places where the bride and groom didn't compromise an inch. The photographer was one. He had photographed many weddings at the site and was intimately familiar with the layout and the lighting. Plus, he was soft-spoken, discreet, and efficient. Later, Michael would say how happy he was to write that thousand-dollar check. Unfortunately, he wasn't as thrilled with the videographer ($1,200) or the band that played for a total of forty-five minutes ($1,200).

With the major logistics out of the way and costs somewhat under control, Padmini and Michael had six months advance time "to try to do a little bit of everything." They began to focus their attention on the dual ceremony, the centerpiece of their wedding.

August 19 was a shimmering sea-blue day on the bluffs, and couldn't have been more perfect for their outdoor wedding. The string quartet began the traditional processional, complete with Michael, his best man (Michael's brother), one bridesmaid (Padmini's sister), two flower girls, and a ring bearer. Everything was in place, including a surprise that Padmini had secretly planned for Michael. She appeared on the arm of her father, wearing the gold-and-ivory silk wedding sari that her mother had bought in India when Padmini was four.

My mom had wanted me to wear the sari the first time I married, but I think I was afraid to be different and

*went for the big elaborate western-style dress instead.
But this time, when I told her what I wanted, it was
her dream come true.*

Padmini's Far Eastern wedding attire was accessorized according to Western tradition. In addition to a short veil, she
wore something old: her maternal grandmother's handker-
chief; something new: a pair of earrings gifted to her by her
mother; something borrowed: a special Sri Lankan wedding
necklace made of semiprecious stones; and something blue:
silk wedding lingerie.

An unknowing Michael was completely taken aback as his
wife-to-be walked lovingly toward him.

*I had never seen her wear anything like that and I was in
total awe. Before we got together, Padmini was sometimes
living a life that other people wanted her to live, and
that isn't what we were going to be about. The sari was
an affirmation, a genuine part of who she is.*

The civil part of Padmini and Michael's ceremony was conducted by a judge, a man Michael knew through his work as
a lawyer and liked for his directness and compassion. As an
officiant, he embodied two other specific characteristics Michael feels are necessary for a lasting marriage: the ability to
recognize one's own faults and the strength to compromise.

Padmini and Michael stood side by side under a simple
arch made of white anthuriums, the national flower of Sri
Lanka, and the judge began the ceremony. He first made a
point of introducing the honored guests who had traveled
long distances to attend. In brief welcoming remarks, he defined the common purpose that had brought these strangers
together: to witness Padmini and Michael's union. Michael recalled the scene.

*Our wedding looked like the UN; we had people from
all over the world. My side is as white as you can*

be after five months of snow in Buffalo, New York.
Padmini's comes in every color. It was a sea of all
kinds of different faces.

In keeping with the couple's emphasis on simplicity, their ceremony was brief. The best man read a poem Padmini had sent Michael early in their courtship: Yeats' "The Valley of Lovers." The bridesmaid read a passage from Kahlil Gibran. And the judge prefaced their vows with a passage from Joseph Campbell describing the *yin* and *yang* of love. Padmini and Michael recited their personal pledges of love and devotion and were pronounced husband and wife.

Then, the newlyweds and their guests made their way from the grounds to the house for a traditional Sri Lankan Oil Lamp Ceremony. Many had no idea what to expect. A five-foot bronze oil lamp, festooned with garlands of jasmine, stood in the center of the vaulted living room. The perfumed air was filled with the sounds of drums and a conch shell being blown.

The newlyweds approached the lamp, hands joined around a single candle. Circling around the multilayered lamp and lighting each descending level, the couple completed this portion of the ritual. With the lamp aglow, Michael then placed the traditional *thali,* a thick gold braid with a medallion, around Padmini's neck. Padmini explained,

The Lamp Ceremony symbolizes unity and the phases
of life. The thali *is very much like a wedding ring.*
Once a husband has placed it there, a wife never
removes it. Traditionally, they are very stiff in the beginning,
but with time, it becomes pliable, just like a marriage.
My mother's is like silk now.

After that, Padmini's eldest sister stepped forward to welcome Michael into their family. One by one, she draped the flower garlands over his bowed head. With the union complete, their dual and unlikely destinies combined, Padmini and Michael sealed the moment in a nontraditional kiss, one that, most definitely, knew no bounds!

Tips from Padmini and Michael

1. Don't listen to anyone who says that different traditions aren't complementary. Feel free to mix and match the rituals that are meaningful to you.

2. Ignore criticism that a mixed tradition wedding might appear "strange" to those who aren't familiar with them. Guests are more adaptable than you think and are thrilled to celebrate in any way that makes *you* happy.

3. Be sure to brief your photographer on what is going to happen just in case he or she has never attended an intercultural wedding. That way the photographer won't miss the crucial moments simply because he or she was unaware of what was coming next.

4. Also, insist that your photographer become familiar with the wedding site and lighting conditions, especially if the celebration is going to take place outdoors.

5. If you rent a site for part of a day, make sure you "schedule" for unexpected delays—they're inevitable. The last thing you want is to shortchange your afternoon wedding because the evening booking is waiting in the wings.

6. If the women in your family are getting their hair done on the day of the wedding at the same salon, make sure they've all booked different hairdressers—or that you, the bride, go first!

7. When you must drive a distance to your wedding site, check driving conditions that day with the highway patrol. Traffic jams occur when you can least afford them.

Retracing Our African Roots:
Lynnette and Akil

The Bride: Age 24, first marriage

The Groom: Age 25, first marriage

Ceremony: Pan-African/Pentecostal

Site: Historic house

Guests: 300

Cost: $8,000

As much as weddings are a threshold to the future, they are also a pathway back to the past. Ritual that revives our ancient origins can help us recover parts of ourselves that have been lost or taken away. Lynnette and Akil set out to accomplish just that when they decided to discard nearly all Western wedding ritual they'd been raised with and draw, instead, from the rich traditions of their historical homeland: Africa. It was a journey that linked their ancient ancestry to themselves, their families, and their community.

Lynnette and Akil felt a deep connection to their African heritage long before they knew one another. As undergraduates in college, each had decided independently that reaffirming their roots would actively influence their lives. Years later, after they had met and decided to marry, that they would have an African wedding was almost an unspoken assumption between them. Akil summed up both of their thoughts on the subject.

Instead of living an "American" or "Eurocentric" life, mine has many aspects that have something to do with my heritage. As I became more aware of my past, I began to celebrate it. African-American psychology talks about the importance of defining your own reality. So having a traditional African wedding was an extension of that.

Although Lynnette and Akil had seen pictures and videos of African-style weddings, neither had actually attended one. Nor had either of their families. That left the couple in charge of creating an authentic celebration capturing "their feel." It also meant a considerable amount of homework was in order. After they had diligently checked out and read stacks of library books on tribal weddings, they consulted with friends, many of whom are from Nigeria, Ethiopia, and Lesotho. The more Lynnette and Akil learned, the greater their appreciation for the startling diversity of African cultural traditions and the complexity of the task before them. Lynnette pointed out,

> *Africa is a huge continent with hundreds of different ethnic groups, customs, and religious and tribal affiliations. Some of the things that we incorporated into our wedding may not necessarily be what someone from Zimbabwe might have done.*
>
> *But combining these different elements into one wedding shows the creativity of all African people. It isn't just an aesthetic thing like "Oh, what a pretty wedding" or "What an original idea." The significance is deep and rich in meaning for us and reflects how we feel about our family and our community. An African wedding isn't just about the joining of two individuals, but that two families are now being united— that's universal.*

After much thought and research, Lynnette and Akil hand-picked the African customs that were meaningful to them and vetoed those that weren't. Neither stood on ceremony.

Because their pluralistic approach required a structure, they retained certain elements of Western weddings: a processional made up of parents, bridesmaids, groomsmen, a ring bearer, and a flower girl. They also registered with a gift registry and Lynnette tossed a bridal bouquet. But it was clear even from the invitations that, despite these familiar touches, this was not going to be just another predictable wedding.

In an announcement letter that preceded the formal invitation, Lynnette and Akil explained that having a traditional African wedding was their attempt to show the central importance of their ancestry in their lives. They shared their commitment to preserving their heritage and invited guests to wear African clothing. The invitation, upon which was stenciled a simple silhouette of the African continent, read: "Together with our families, Lynnette and Akil invite you to share in the traditional African wedding ceremony uniting us in marriage."

Immediately, invited guests were abuzz with anticipation and reactions. One friend told Lynnette, "I don't understand why you have to have an African wedding. You're an American now." More important, some members of the couple's respective families were skeptical or ill at ease with the idea. Akil understood their discomfort.

Many African-Americans perceive Africans the same way that European-Americans do. They share many of the same images, so they're looking for Tarzan with a bone through his nose. Even my grandfather told me he was worried that somebody was going to show up in a loincloth.

But even if that were the case, there's this whole idea of rejecting your past and trying to embrace something that rejects you. That's the dichotomy that people are trying to deal with.

Lynnette and Akil asked that everyone in the wedding party wear traditional African garb. Initially, their request met with some resistance, especially from the fathers who feared they would feel awkward arrayed in the generously draped Nigerian apparel stitched from luminous gold fabrics. Their concerns, however, were short-lived. One fitting convinced them that the clothing was flattering and felt natural.

Another temporary obstacle concerned finances, because the bride and groom were paying for a large part of the wedding themselves. With so many guests invited, initial plans for a sit-down luncheon were scaled back to tasty North African finger-foods: falafel balls, fried plantain, okra. Lynnette's mother offered to prepare fifty whole chickens, American-style, with greens and potato salad.

As their wedding day approached, several standard prenuptial parties were given in the couple's honor: an all-female shower for Lynnette, a bachelor party for Akil, and a coed "couple shower" hosted by Akil's mother. All of these get-togethers were wonderful, but one was particularly noteworthy. To round out the prewedding events, Lynnette and Akil added a long-standing Lesotho custom: parental prewedding counseling during which family members assemble to "say their piece" to the bride and groom.

This gathering is an opportunity for elders to share their own marital mistakes and experience and for newlyweds-to-be to listen and learn. The formalized exchange defines the boundaries of the new extended family. In-laws begin to know one another, and lines of communication between the new couple are established.

Although Lynnette and Akil are well aware of the importance of an open dialogue in their own relationship, a meeting designed to draw on and be instructed by the experience of older adults is rare in our culture. For the bride and groom, hearing their parents' insights was beneficial as well as auspicious.

Our parents talked for at least a couple of hours and it was good advice—what to do and what not to do. Both sides of marriage were represented—from my mother who is divorced and from Akil's parents who have been married over twenty-five years. They talked a lot about understanding, tolerance, and acceptance of the person even when you want to just wring their neck. And they invited us to come to them with any concerns or problems we might have.

Shortly thereafter, Lynnette and Akil's wedding took place in the lush garden of a Victorian manor house owned by an African-American women's organization. Choosing this particular wedding site was one more expression of the bride and groom's community spirit: apart from the manor's stately beauty, the rental costs benefited a student scholarship fund.

Live African drummers signaled arriving guests that the wedding processional was about to begin. A hush fell over the crowd when the 14-member wedding party appeared, dressed in dazzling shades of green, gold, and burnished orange. Leading the processional was the best man, who carried a large woven basket laden with gifts comprising the "bride price"—the dowry the husband-to-be traditionally bestows on the bride's family in many African cultures. Akil had selected each memento with much care.

In Africa, you give yams or cattle or something of that nature. I wasn't going to do that, but we did do things to represent bride price. I gave both mothers bracelets from the Ivory Coast and Lynnette's mother a handwoven scarf from Kenya. Her father and uncle received bronze Sphinx statues. And for Lynnette, a handmade Egyptian jewelry box containing jewelry.

The groom was dressed in a mint-green Nigerian *abada*, a four-piece ensemble with matching hat, ornately embroidered along the edges in gold. Akil added a personal touch, an Ethiopian ornamental fly swat made of a goat's tail. "It made me feel like royalty," he said with a grin.

When Akil reached the altar, he turned to see Lynnette escorted on one side by her father and on the other by her father's brother. The music shifted from the drumming to "Bring Me Joy," a song recorded by Diane Reeves, a popular jazz artist. The upbeat Afro-Caribbean rhythm, captured Lynnette's deepest hopes and wishes for her upcoming marriage.

Diane Reeves' music is very touching and meaningful.
In Swahili, the title of this song is "Fumilayo." The first
lyric is "Allah, bring me joy." And to me it was almost
like a prayer. The drums start playing and after that, the
music becomes very celebratory. I said to myself, "God,
make everything be okay, make everything work out."

Lynnette's attire was as strikingly regal as Akil's. Her dress, a
two-tiered full-length African-style wrap, was created from a
generous swath of mint-green silk that matched Akil's *abada*.
And like him, she wore sandals. Unlike her bridesmaids, she
did not wear a head wrap.

But a mint-green wedding dress hadn't always been
Lynnette's first choice. Initially, she had purchased several
yards of white brocade, thinking she would have the best of
both worlds: an African-style dress made of "traditional" white.
However, once her cultural blinders were off, she changed her
mind.

I was holding on to something psychological, like "A white
dress is what you wear, no matter what kind of
wedding we have." Maybe it was how I grew up or
thinking my mom wanted me to walk down the aisle
that way.
    But then I just thought about all my bridesmaids
and ushers wearing colors and how I would really
look out of place. A white dress was not in keeping with
the whole image of a traditional African wedding. When
I made the decision to change it, I never regretted it.
Not once.

The wedding ceremony was co-officiated by a Pentecostal
minister and a traditional African officiant. Shaheed, the African officiant, began the wedding ritual by asking the elders
for permission to perform the ceremony. Voices and applause
rang out in affirmation. Once he had gotten the go-ahead, he
chanted an Arabic prayer and asked that the couple light a

Unity Candle, referencing the Swahili concept of *umoja*, the first of seven principles from the *Nguzo Saba*.

Next, the Pentecostal minister joined the bride and groom on the altar and spoke at length about the challenge of commitment. The couple exchanged the vows each had written separately, and then they simultaneously recited one paragraph promising that "Divorce is not an option."

With this portion of the ceremony completed, Shaheed invited all the family members to come up to the altar. In this moment of togetherness, the names of long-departed familial ancestors were called out and given tribute. These acts of honoring and respecting the past symbolized the wedding's essence: that two families and many generations were becoming one, not just two individuals. This moment, according to Lynnette, embodied everything she and Akil had hoped to express.

> *It was simply a way to say thank you to the people who came before us and had made it possible for me to be with the man I love, to have an opportunity to pursue my education and career, to have a fulfilled life. A lot of these people really didn't get to do what they wanted because they were struggling so much just to maintain their families and to overcome prejudice.*
>
> *After the ceremony, my Uncle Sonny, who had been very uneasy with our plans, took me aside. He said, "I just wanted to tell you that this was one of the most beautiful weddings, and I really appreciated it." Just that look on his face, I knew that he meant it and I knew that he understood, finally, what I was trying to do: that I very much appreciate my heritage and wanted to incorporate that into a wedding that reflected who I am.*

A jubilant reception followed, alive with the sounds of Nigerian music, African drummers, jazz, and a musical piece written by Akil's uncle. Guests passed the afternoon dancing and eating. Near its end, a wedding cake in the shape of two pyramids with an *ankh* atop was unveiled. The *ankh*, the Egyptian symbol of life, captured the spirit of Lynnette and Akil's union precisely. In Akil's words,

> *We embraced our own background and grounded ourselves*
> *in our beliefs, despite opposition. As a couple, we*
> *learned that we are both dedicated to our values.*
> *Planning this wedding took fortitude and perseverance.*
> *There is a saying in the African tradition and that is*
> *that if you have knowledge about something and you*
> *don't use it, you're better off being a cow, because*
> *at least when you die your flesh can be eaten. Lynnette*
> *and I want to nourish ourselves and our community with*
> *knowledge. That was our objective for the wedding*
> *and I think that we accomplished it.*

Tips from Lynnette and Akil

1. Most of us can trace our roots to other countries and traditions. Don't be afraid to explore and celebrate your heritage at your wedding by combining diverse elements that represent more accurately who you are and where you have come from.

2. Educate yourself about your heritage and the possibilities of incorporating aspects of it into your ceremony. Do research and consult authoritative sources.

3. There is no "right" way or "wrong" way to plan a wedding. Don't limit yourself by thinking "It has always been done this way" or "Everybody in my family always does it this way."

4. Experiment, but be guided by what speaks most directly to your hearts.

5. Stay the course and resist the pressure to please relatives or friends who may not agree with you.

Interfaith Weddings

Interfaith marriages are those that unite couples of different denominations or religious faiths. The central issue from a theological perspective turns on whether or not two people who don't share the same belief system can enter into a valid religious contract of marriage. Some of the world's major religions have taken a position on this complicated question that affects millions of couples. The ideological differences are considerable, as the following summary from *Modern Bride's Guide to Your Wedding & Marriage* (New York: Ballantine, 1984) indicates:

Buddhist: Marriage is a civil matter not outlined in Buddhist scripture. A monk traditionally blesses the couple before or after the ceremony, but interfaith marriage is not a religious issue.

Hinduism: Interfaith marriage is not advocated, but does take place under certain circumstances. Check with the pujari (Hindu priest).

Judaism: Strict Judaic law does not recognize the validity of a contract between a Jew and a non-Jew. Some Reform rabbis, however, will perform an interfaith ceremony.

Mormon: Mormons may marry outside the faith, but if they do, they may not marry in a Mormon temple. Since marriage is forever, into eternity, divorce is unthinkable.

Moslem: The Koran, the book of Islamic law, classifies Moslems, Christians, and Jews as believers in the true God and therefore acceptable for intermarriage. By extension, a Moslem may also marry a practicing Buddhist or Hindu.

Eastern Orthodox: Interfaith marriage is not encouraged but a dispensation may be granted provided the nonorthodox party is a Christian baptized in the name of the Holy Trinity.

Protestant: Some conservative Protestant groups will not perform a marriage between a Protestant and a non-Christian, and the Episcopal Church has rules about divorce and remarriage. Check with the minister of your denomination.

Roman Catholic: Routine dispensations are granted for a Catholic to marry someone of another faith, Christian or not, provided that each person is considered free to marry by the Roman Catholic Church. Each case is handled on an individual basis, so check with the priest.

The extent to which an interdenominational or interfaith couple can expect to represent their specific traditions in one ceremony with one officiant, depends on the clergyperson conducting it. Often it is left to the discretion of the officiant to determine if and how a couple will be wed. For example, some Protestant pastors gladly adapt the liturgy so that both Christian and Jewish traditions are affirmed in the wedding, including musical selections, particular prayers, and Hebrew Scriptures. However, it is more difficult to find a rabbi who will do the same. Only about half of the Reform and Reconstructionist rabbis are willing to marry an interreligious couple.

Harder still is finding co-officiants to conduct an "ecumenical" worship service, one in which a rabbi participates, together with a priest or minister. The key to overcoming this obstacle is persistence. Be prepared to make many calls. Consult Reformed rabbis; if they aren't willing to co-officiate, they may be able to direct you to a rabbi or cantor who is. Or ask friends who know other interfaith couples to connect you so you can ask them how they went about locating their officiants. Willing Jewish officiants *are* out there, but not in great numbers. Hang in there—it's worth it!

Irrespective of whether an interfaith couple wishes to have a single or co-officiated ceremony, interfaith weddings challenge individuals to clarify their personal relationship to their own faith as well as examine issues that will resonate profoundly throughout their married relationship. Important questions that invariably surface are: How will each spouse define his or her relationship to the other's faith and observance? How will the couple celebrate religious holidays? What kind of religious nurture will children receive? How will in-laws be included?

It is helpful if a couple is willing to engage in careful reflection and open discussion with their spiritual advisers concerning these and other questions. How open each is to articulating concerns and fears about these issues reveals much about the couple's ability to communicate. Hearing and understanding the other's devout beliefs is a learning process. Sorting out the particulars of an interfaith wedding is excellent preparation for a couple's ongoing dialogue—one that is critical to maintaining the future health of the marriage.

Apart from all the longer-term issues mentioned earlier, certain practical questions must be answered concerning the wedding. Among the most important: Will it be held in a house of worship? On what day and at what time? Who will officiate? How will the respective wedding rituals, symbols, and customs be incorporated into one ceremony? How will specific food restrictions, religious music, and special attire be decided upon? How should family and friends who are uncomfortable with combining different theologies into one ceremony be handled?

There are no hard and fast rules concerning these details; much is left to the conscience and creativity of the spouses-to-be. Moreover, the outcome will depend on the depth of each person's devotion to his or her respective faith. Other considerations include: whether or not each is actively affiliated with a religious congregation, the degree of family pressure to conform to set rituals, and the flexibility of the co-officiants.

Much controversy surrounds the risks and challenges of interfaith weddings and the potential difficulty of arranging interfaith marriages. But are they fundamentally different than those in which husband and wife share a common faith? Rabbi Ted Falcon, who has worked with interfaith couples and co-officiated scores of ecumenical ceremonies, thinks not.

Terribly difficult issues come up with any *wedding and I am unconvinced that co-officiated weddings are any*

*more difficult. Sometimes they actually make things
clearer because a couple is forced to become aware
of just one of the differences that they have going into
a marriage. If a couple is able to successfully cope with
that difference, it bodes well for the other differences
they will discover in their marriage.*

Keeping the Faith: The Rabbi, The Minister, and the Texas Swing Band: Leslie and Mark

The Bride:	Age 30, second marriage
The Groom:	Age 41, first marriage
Ceremony:	Christian/Jewish
Site:	Rented estate
Guests:	90
Cost:	$30,000

If what Rabbi Falcon says is true, then Leslie and Mark, a couple who identify with their respective faiths, are on their way to building a lasting marriage. She's Lutheran. He's Jewish. Both wanted to intermingle and balance the key elements of their separate religious traditions in their wedding ceremony while still preserving the integrity of each. Quite soon, they realized this was a tall order but one that they eventually accomplished with grace and artistry.

Mark's Christmas Day proposal to Leslie and imminent wedding, prompted him to reexplore his connection to his "lapsed" faith. Over twenty years had passed since his bar mitzvah and during this time his active participation in Judaism had faded. But these distant memories of his upbringing stirred as he matured. As he moved closer to marriage, he thought more seriously about reaffirming his religious ties. After searching for a spiritual home, Mark decided to reaffiliate with a Jewish congregation whose Reform rabbi held eclectic, liberal views that were consonant with his own.

Leslie, too, hadn't actively practiced her religion after she had become an adult. This was in stark contrast to her formative years. The daughter of a Lutheran pastor, she had regularly participated in church activities. Lutheran teachings and practice were a focal point of her life. Although she still enjoys services when she visits her parents, she rarely attends on her own except for Easter and Christmas holidays.

It wasn't until Mark renewed his interest in Judaism that Leslie began to reexamine her relationship to her own faith. And while she accompanied Mark to synagogue, she realized that she had to find "a spiritual place that was mine or be left out." At the moment, Leslie isn't seeking to rejoin a Lutheran church, yet the process of planning her interfaith wedding rekindled connections to her upbringing that she wants to preserve.

Mark and Leslie both know that the key to achieving their "separate togetherness" is to respect each other's differences, profoundly and completely. Yet, even with all good intentions, this is often more easily accomplished in theory than in practice. As the couple began to jointly shape their interfaith ceremony, they occasionally disagreed. An equitable balance wasn't always so simple to achieve, especially in emotional terms. But, according to Leslie, the process also brought them closer together.

It was a lesson in not being defensive and trying to be really receptive, understanding, and respectful of the other person's background. I think that Mark and I were especially careful when it came to giving each other a lot of room. We could say anything and have our fears, but we knew that we had to honor what was important to the other person.

Both knew that finding the right co-officiants for their interfaith ceremony was a critical element to each partner's satis-
faction. As mentioned earlier, Christian clergy are more open
to co-officiating interfaith marriages, whereas willing Jewish
clergy are more difficult to find—but not in Leslie and Mark's
case. Leslie's father put her in touch with a pastor, his long-
time colleague, who agreed to co-officiate her wedding without any reservations. Mark was also fortunate, because the
rabbi from his congregation is one of the few in his city who
willingly performs co-officiated weddings. However, before
making any final choices, the couple met with the rabbi and
the pastor alone several times.

The next step was to make sure that the co-officiants would
complement each other and work well together so Leslie and
Mark invited the rabbi and the pastor to meet over lunch.
Providence was on their side. Both men were genuinely excited by each other's ideas and seemed to approach the idea
of a Lutheran/Jewish wedding without prejudices. Mark recalled the clergymen's instant chemistry: "One of them would
say, 'Here is what I would do . . .,' and then the other would
say, 'That's great, I'm going to use that!'" Surprisingly, they
were receptive of, even enthusiastic about, Mark and Leslie's
unorthodox symbolism. Leslie explained:

> We were trying to think of symbols for Christianity and
> symbols for Judaism. The chuppah is a very visible
> symbol and so is the cross. The idea was this: four
> crosses bearing the Jewish tallis [prayer shawl] that
> represented the two of us, of different faiths, standing hand
> in hand.

Unlike the open-minded co-officiants, a handful of close
friends and relatives who were told in advance of the *chuppah*
made of crosses and a *tallis,* were offended. Leslie's father emphatically cautioned her against it, insisting, "You don't want
to mix the two." Similarly, one of Mark's distant cousins told
him outright that uniting the symbols was an affront to his

Jewish sensibilities. Someone else called the idea "blasphe-mous."

At the heart of these bruised feelings was the proximity of the Christian crosses to the Jewish prayer shawl. Having them in the same ceremony was acceptable, but having them actu-ally touching seemed to evoke an onslaught of criticism. These reactions couldn't help but disturb Leslie and Mark. Af-ter much back and forth on the subject, Mark posed a rhetor-ical question to Leslie: "If it is so wrong for two distinct symbols to be side by side, then must *we* also stand a certain distance apart at the altar?" Leslie thought for a moment and then said, "Yeah, screw 'em, they're wrong!" The realization put the "chuppah issue" to rest and the couple commissioned two artist friends, a weaver and a sculptor, to design and cre-ate what was to be the most controversial part of their cere-mony.

Yet, amid all the agreement, Leslie occasionally felt "edged out" by the Jewish elements of the ceremony. Initially, she per-ceived the *chuppah* or wedding canopy, the yarmulkas, and the *tallis* as more "colorful" and "visually dramatic" than the Christian symbols. At one point, Leslie even suggested intro-ducing liturgical music played on a pipe organ as a balance, but because the ceremony was to be held outside, this idea proved impractical.

But the parity Leslie was seeking was really internal and emotional, and the wedding ceremony simply mirrored her growing sense of powerlessness vis à vis Mark. Once she real-ized that she wasn't going to be emotionally overwhelmed un-less *she* permitted that to happen, she felt on equal footing once again.

Much of what I experienced was my tendency to feel invisible or smaller in the face of what looks huge or set. I came into contact with my needing to fight more for my place. Under other circumstances, I might have gotten married in a church, and that would have cinched the

Christianity and it wouldn't have caused me to look deeper.

As soon as Leslie and Mark had cleared these difficult emotional hurdles, the more routine aspects of wedding planning seemed comparatively "easy." The couple agreed to finance their wedding together and take full responsibility for planning it. After all, Leslie's family had paid for her first wedding and she wouldn't consider allowing them to pay for anything the second time around. Mark, who was marrying for the first time at age forty-one, felt he was responsible for himself as well. Their "joint venture," was nearly fifty–fifty. Leslie, who was in graduate school at the time, contributed ten thousand dollars from her savings, Mark's parents insisted on giving the couple a generous gift of five thousand dollars, and Mark, a writer, covered the rest.

Another "easy" decision involved wedding gifts. Leslie had been married before, so she wasn't inclined to ask for gifts, let alone register. Mark, who had never married but had lived independently for years, agreed. As an alternative, the couple requested that guests make donations to Save the Children or Greenpeace, two organizations they actively support.

Besides, Leslie and Mark were far more interested in giving than receiving so why not host an elegant wedding set in extraordinary surroundings, far removed from everyone's daily experience, as a gift to the people they loved? They envisioned a location that was self-contained and low-keyed so that the out-of-town families could relax and get to know one another, almost as if they were on vacation. The newlyweds-to-be conceived the perfect solution: rent a rambling estate with grounds and a pool for an entire twenty-four hours.

Their ambitious plan was this: host a casual picnic starting at 11:00 A.M. poolside, complete with umbrellas, coolers, and lounge chairs. Swim, play volleyball and croquet all afternoon. Snack from tables laden with everything from deli to peanut butter for the kids. By 3:30 P.M. have guests return to their hotels via prearranged shuttles. Allow for a few unhurried hours to spruce up and be back at the estate by 6:30 P.M. for the wedding ceremony. Reception to follow including sit-down dinner and dancing to a Texas swing band late into the night.

Because Mark was scheduled to be out of town a great deal during the five months that preceded the wedding, Leslie took care of most of the arrangements. Fortunately, one of her friends is a professional event planner who insisted on helping and waived her usual fee. Luckier still, Leslie's friend called in "favors" and received substantial cost reductions on everything from the valet parking company to the seamstress.

Yet, even with the help, organizing the festivities was far from effortless. Leslie and Mark have distinct work styles and rhythms. First, the couple discovered that they weren't always interested in the same planning details or sharing every decision. For example, while Mark was completely engaged in the design of their invitations, Leslie was immersed in planning the menu and selecting the photographer. Ultimately, they decided that whoever cared about detail X or Y the most deserved to have it their way and needed to make it their responsibility. With that understood, the planning process went from being like a "three-legged race" to one that built trust and confidence.

Then there were issues about scheduling. Mark considered five months a long time, and so his planning pace was "fairly leisurely." Leslie, who considers herself more detail-oriented, tended to "adrenalize!" At moments, Leslie felt they "were on a bicycle built for two: I was in the front speeding and Mark was applying the brakes simultaneously!" Much of this tension was diluted by the event planner. Just the fact that the couple could make the major decisions, then let the details be handled by someone else was a relief. And, of course, as the date approached, things fell into place.

A nearly imperceptible breeze and cloudless sky graced the Sunday of the wedding. From the back of the garden came the soft jingling of camel bells, as the wedding canopy was carried down the aisle by Leslie's younger sister, Mark's younger brother, and the couple's two best friends. It was a sight no one had ever seen before.

Four variations of the cross standing more than eight feet high supported the billowing Jewish prayer cloth, handwoven and containing one errant red thread. The thread had been Mark's idea and expressed his "spirit of rebelliousness." The front set of wooden poles, flanking Leslie and Mark, were carved in the form of two elongated nude figures on crossbars. The male was entwined by four snakes; the female, in roses. Their arms were stretched upward in the *tadasana* yoga pose that Leslie and Mark practice daily. The set of crosses in the back was more free-form, reminiscent of wind-filled tree branches, sacred and wild.

The wedding procession began with an ecumenical selection of music performed by several of the couple's musician friends: a Hassidic song, a Bach liturgical hymn, and a special song composed by Mark himself. Mark and both parents, one on each side, made their way to the altar. Leslie, accompanied by her parents, followed.

In keeping with Christian protocol, the bride stood at the groom's left, a unity candle burning before them. Both wore white. Leslie's two-tiered dress, one she had designed herself, had a removable long tulip skirt for the ceremony with a short skirt underneath for the reception. Mark wore oatmeal-colored trousers, a shirt secured at the collar by a large moonstone, and a colorful African skullcap "that looked like a crown."

The ceremony that followed was a deliberate interweaving of both Christian and Jewish elements, kept in balance by the sensitivity and cooperation of the co-officiants. Both men had joined together with one goal in mind: to spiritually assist the harmonious union of the couple and their families. The rabbi began by drawing attention to the obvious—the wedding canopy. "Before we start," he said, "I just have to say that I can't imagine a more appropriate symbol for what we are doing here today." He proceeded to welcome everyone.

Then Leslie's father stood up and delivered a Lutheran blessing over the couple. The rabbi followed with a blessing and led both sets of parents in a critical sequence leading up to the marriage vows, in which they were asked to endorse and support the couple's separate togetherness. It was a moment Mark remembers vividly.

> *The rabbi had our parents stand and then he said something like, "Do you pledge yourself to honor your children's marriage and respect the integrity of their beliefs and acknowledge their independence?" When my parents said yes, they were saying, in effect, "Yes, Leslie is Christian and we honor and support that." And Leslie's parents were saying, "Yes, Mark is Jewish and we honor and support that."*

The Lutheran pastor then asked the guests to rise and make the same promise. As soon as they took their seats, both co-officiants began reading the marriage vows. The couple did not write their own, but edited a version collated by the rabbi and pastor, some of which was based on shared Old Testament text but spoken in English, not Hebrew. Minor word changes requested by the bride and groom were made beforehand by the co-officiants, who made sure that neither compromised the essential elements of their respective traditions. Hebrew blessings were included, together with references to Jesus, the Father, the Son, and The Holy Spirit.

Following the marriage vows, the rabbi gave the Seven Benedictions. After the blessing of the wine, the bride and groom drank from a common chalice, a practice present in both Christianity and Judaism. Next came the ring exchange. Mark's rabbi led him in both Aramaic and English pledging, "With this ring you are consecrated to me as my wife according to the traditions of my faith and to all I hold most holy." Leslie, led by the Lutheran pastor, spoke these same words to Mark in English only. Another set of blessings was made by the rabbi in Hebrew and by the pastor in English.

With the glass-breaking, as is customary in the Jewish tradition, Leslie and Mark were pronounced husband and wife.

The couple eagerly sealed the vows with *two* non-denominational kisses—the first on the urging of the rabbi, the second of the pastor!

The evening reception followed under the starry night sky. Guests enjoyed buffets of Italian, California, or Indonesian cuisine and delighted in three whimsical wedding cakes: oversized replicas of a Hostess Twinkie, Cupcake, and Snowball! They twirled and two-stepped to the music of a live Texas swing band. Toasts and roasts were made.

Then Leslie's sister Karen presented the newlyweds with their first gift as husband and wife: a wedding quilt. For months preceding the wedding, unbeknownst to Leslie or Mark, wedding guests contributed pieces of fabric from the couple's pasts—a scrap from Mark's great uncle's tablecloth, a swatch from Leslie's best friend's wedding dress. The patchwork of the distinct memories and mementos of the couple's lives echoed their wedding ceremony, which had interlaced disparate sacred elements to sanctify their bond.

Theirs was a celebration of love as well as a determination to represent their most inner selves, authentically, with as few compromises as possible. Looking back, Leslie and Mark realize that the challenges of planning their interfaith wedding foreshadow some of the challenges they will face in their marriage, especially when they decide to have children. Yet, they believe that having acknowledged their differences and having bridged them, they are better prepared for what may come. On this point, Mark speaks for both of them.

> *The connections we have with our respective faiths are connected with our feeling for family. When I was living with my family, I was happy to go to the synagogue because I was with them. And Leslie felt the same way about her family.*
>
> *So it makes sense that now that she and I have become a two-person family, both of us are longing for those childhood comforts. They have become more*

important. We're no longer comets circling the sun, we're now entering a solar system.

Tips from Leslie and Mark

1. Use this time for careful self-examination and to clarify your own beliefs. You might uncover parts of yourself that you didn't know existed or discover changes you weren't aware of.

2. Honor your mate's faith as you honor your own. Try to learn as much as you can about their religion. Mutual understanding enhances every wedding and marriage.

3. Talk, talk, talk. Bring your secret fears about marrying into another faith out into the open. Speaking these thoughts aloud often diffuses them.

4. Don't silently compromise your most ardent wishes or cover up your concerns. These resentments can spill into your marriage and cause trouble later.

5. Think of your interfaith wedding as a big jigsaw puzzle. If you can't get all the pieces to fit, try juxtaposing them differently.

6. Find co-officiants who are as open-minded as you are. Don't use anyone who tries to undermine your attempts to fairly balance your interfaith ceremony. Work with them to craft the kind of ceremony *you* want!

7. If you are having difficulty finding a rabbi to co-officiate an interfaith wedding, call a local Reform Temple and ask for a referral or contact: Rabbinic Intermarriage Counseling, Rabbi Irwin Fishbein, 128 East Dudley Avenue, Westfield, NJ 07090; 201-233-0419.

8. But don't expect approval from everyone. Squabbles and bruised feelings are often inevitable. In the face of resistance, maintain a sense of humor and, most important, a sense of compassion for those who aren't open-minded enough to accept your views.

9. Excellent books devoted exclusively to the subject are available in your library or local bookstores. Read whatever you can on the subject, but be discerning!

Differences that Make a Difference

Planning a wedding that embraces a couple's religious or cultural differences and similarities requires that the bride and groom honestly examine their distinct spiritual and cultural identities. By asking yourselves questions like: Who am I? What do I/we want to be? What does this wedding mean to me? How do I want the ceremony and celebration to reflect my background? you'll be taking the first steps toward successfully fusing each perspective into one highly original wedding ceremony.

As the answers to these questions become clarified, they should be enfolded into the specific structure and content of the ceremony. After a couple knows what they want, officiants, with their expertise, can translate these spiritual objectives into ritual. Padmini and Michael decided on two back-to-back ceremonies that were freestanding and complete unto themselves. Lynnette and Akil combined African customs from many sources with Western ones to produce one unique ceremonial blend. And Leslie and Mark interwove Judeo-Christian elements into a single ritual that counterbalanced the two traditions.

Crafting new ceremonial ground is venturesome and exciting. On the one hand, anything that strays from convention is open to criticism and judgment. But on the other, unpredictability can be enlivening—blended ceremonies catch people off guard. More often than not, those bearing witness are mesmerized and deeply touched by the authentic expression of a couple's most inner selves.

Beauty and integrity are interwoven in the process of becoming who we are as individuals and who we can become as husband and wife. If you have any doubts about the "rightness" of an intercultural or interfaith wedding, keep the words of Rabbi Ted Falcon in mind: "Each human being is carrying a spark, no matter what he or she believes, no matter what their color, or the language one uses. God doesn't speak one language. God speaks every language at once."

All weddings consecrate the universal aspects of identity and the spiritual ideal of oneness. And for that simple reason, each and every one is sacred.

CHAPTER 5

Imaginations Run Wild

*What lies behind us and what lies before us are
tiny matters compared to what lies within us.*
—Emerson

What do the following events have in common? A child
builds a miniature castle using oatmeal boxes and milk
cartons. A gourmet cook prepares a cheese and leek soufflé
without a recipe. Two architectural students choose their favorite art-deco building for their wedding site and transport
their guests back to the 1930s via wedding attire, music, and
decor.

In one word, the answer is *creativity.* Creativity is part of everyone's innate potential, a perk that automatically comes
with being human. Harnessing this natural inventiveness involves recognizing what already exists and not being afraid to
tap into it. It really is quite simple: we need only give ourselves the time and space to listen to our creative spirit, to
release the imaginative muse that resides within us all.

The imaginative weddings chronicled in this chapter are examples of how inspired couples can allow their inner, intuitive
voices to guide them. Not unlike the artist who sets about
painting a landscape she has never seen, or a musician com-
posing a song he has never heard, these brides and grooms

honored and awakened their "wedding muse." In doing so, they prove that a wedding doesn't have to be solemn, formal, or predictable to be sacred or transcendent. In fact, there is no reason why spontaneity, improvisation, humor, and fun can't be as much a part of the design of a wedding as taking the marriage vows. To surprise, enchant, astonish, and involve begets joy—the prime ingredient that every wedding strives for.

Couples who plan creative weddings do so because they feel that traditional celebrations fall woefully short of expressing who they are and what their relationship stands for. Not wanting to quash their independent urges, they take chances with the tried and tested formulas. That way they aren't locked in by all the vexing details required by proper "wediquette," and can decide for themselves what stays and what goes. The bottom line: these newlyweds-to-be dare to be and delight in being different.

But before we explore this topic further, allow us to make one important distinction. The imaginative weddings we are about to discuss are *not* the bizarre events we frequently hear about on the local nightly news or read about in *People* magazine. Topless weddings, underwater weddings, Laundromat weddings are in a category of their own and hold special significance for those who conceive them. But few of us are likely to go to these extremes or stretch the boundaries of wedding ritual this far. So if you want advice about how to stage your processional on a pair of African elephants lumbering down the Atlantic City boardwalk or exchange vows bungee-jumping 175 feet, you'll have to look elsewhere. But if you're intrigued by the possibility of having a wedding that creatively expresses who you are and how you feel about your spouse-to-be, read on.

A Fresh Look

The first step in planning an inventive wedding is de-programming your cultural expectations of what a wedding is supposed to look like. Try to envision the event from a new perspective. For example, guests might be asked to shift their role from passive witnesses to participants who will join the ceremony. Or an officiant may be called upon to function more as a principal to further the creative theme of the celebration and less as a vested authority who "sanctions" the marriage. More unusual still, the setting and activities associated with the event may not be "wedding-ish" in the least.

Here is a sampling of some imaginative weddings we'd love to have been invited to. Jenny and Steve hosted a "How We Fell in Love Wedding" that literally retraced the meeting places of their early courtship in one evening. Forty-four guests were instructed to rendezvous at a friend's house on the appointed Saturday afternoon, dressed for a night on the town! Everyone boarded a chartered bus, complete with a professional driver, yummy hors d'oeuvres, and an excellent sound system. Their first stop: the neighborhood Irish pub, where Jenny and Steve first met. Several champagne toasts later, the wedding party reboarded the bus and continued on to their second destination, a Mexican cantina. Mariachis serenaded the wedding wayfarers just as they had when Jenny and Steve had dined there on their second date. Over the next two hours, guests were treated to a never-ending stream of spicy house specialties prepared in honor of the bride and groom.

For the last leg of the wedding caravan, guests were transported to a downtown dance club, the site of the couple's third date. The wedding party was directed to a reserved private room where a friend, who was also a justice of the peace, conducted Jenny and Steve's secular vows. Champagne and a luscious chocolate-mousse wedding cake was served. Then, in a high-spirited recessional, the newlyweds led their guests out onto the main dance floor where they had first danced the night away two years before!

Just-marrieds Cassidy and Rick combined a "How We Met Wedding" with their favorite sport: skiing. Their wedding took place on a mountain crest during a full moon at the height of the winter solstice. The avid skiers arranged for a local clergyman, a devoted skier himself, to officiate atop the ski run. Gondolas transported the bride and groom—Cassidy in a white bodysuit with a fur-trimmed hood and Rick in black—and thirty of their ski buddies to the summit.

The wedding party strapped on their skis and schussed halfway down the slope until they reached a snow-frosted grove of pine trees. Guests formed a candlelit crescent around the couple as they whispered their vows.

In the silence of the snow flurries, Cassidy and Rick skied down the mountain alone together, leaving their guests temporarily behind. Within minutes, all were reunited in the cozy Swiss chalet where hot-mulled wine and cheese fondues awaited them, together with the rest of their less-adventurous friends. A hearty alpine dinner followed, filled with laughter, firelight, and a cache of gifts from the bridal registry they'd set up at their favorite ski shop!

Imaginative weddings can also be based on holidays other than Valentine's Day, Christmas Eve, or New Year's Eve—the most obvious ones—or the birthdays of famous people. Consider these:

- A bride and groom engineered a "Halloween/Surprise Wedding Party," asking their unsuspecting guests to come in costume and then showing up as a real-life bride and groom and taking for-real vows!
- A couple, both opera buffs and Mozart fans, arranged to be married on the stage set of *The Marriage of Figaro* on the composer's birthday. The small-town opera company attended and sang selections from their favorite arias.

A natural flair for unusual and unconventional ways of doing things are the grist of imaginative weddings. But as far as they may stray from standardized wedding protocol, there are limits. Certain ritual fundamentals remain in place so that no one will confuse the celebration with a sweet-sixteen party or a clambake!

All marriage ceremonies in the West are built on three common elements: a verbal promise of mutual commitment, the exchange of objects that symbolizes the pledge (i.e., rings), and a physical act that seals the vows (i.e., a kiss)—all in the presence of an officiant and at least one witness. Once these barest essentials are present, just about anything goes! And it does. Creative couples are bound only by the limits of their imaginations, and, as we will see, those limits are endless.

All the Guests Wore White: Samantha and Craig

The Bride:	Age 50, second marriage, 2 sons, ages 23 and 25.
The Groom:	Age 38, first marriage
Ceremony:	Nondenominational
Site:	Their backyard
Guests:	82
Cost:	$8,000

After eight years of living together, Samantha and Craig decided to marry. The first tip-off that theirs was not to be a typical wedding was their announcement that arrived nearly a year before the projected date. Across the background of a hand-colored, color-photocopied photomontage of the couple on St. Eustatius in the Netherlands Antilles was playfully scrawled, "Announcing our intention to be married in a Summer *Nupital* Event."

No, *nupital* was not a misprint. Craig had coined the word

as an off-center alternative to the conventional, if not stiff-sounding, "nuptial." In fact, the whole announcement was intended to set the tone for the wedding to come. Craig explained.

> *As a result of our union there is creativity. We wanted our wedding to symbolize the life-giving aspects of our relationship in such a way that attending it would be an enlivening experience for our guests. So a lot of the wedding was designed to evoke the creativity that we possess as a result of being together.*

Sending the announcements so far in advance and mailing them all on the same day in plain manila envelopes accomplished several things at once: it eliminated the problem of who-got-told-first, caught people by surprise, and piqued everyone's curiosity. Most important, a long lead time allowed the couple to carefully plan the "performance art piece," which was to become their wedding.

"To be alive in marriage is crucial for me," Samantha stressed emphatically, "so we wanted our wedding to be playful, full of music and fun. We started from scratch and asked, 'What do *we* want?' "

The canvas upon which they could let their imaginations run wild is located, conveniently enough, in their own backyard. Tiers of ferns and thick, spongy grass sheltered by tall eucalyptus lead down to a small running stream. It is nothing less than an enchanted glade; a natural setting for a Gatsby-like lawn party.

Although the property could accommodate any number of guests, Craig and Samantha's first instinct was to have a small wedding, family and close friends only. Because both partners are older and less concerned about pleasing others, they avoided inviting people just because they were "supposed to or because feelings might be hurt." Nevertheless, the process was painstaking. Whittling down the guest list was sometimes difficult, and the couple didn't always agree. Samantha described how she and Craig dealt with these impasses.

> *What we had to do was to state our position about inviting*
> *someone and why that person was important to us.*
> *We had an impasse a couple of times and when that*
> *happened we walked away from it. Then, coming back*
> *with a clear head, we could compromise.*

Once the guest list was agreed upon, they got down to the fun of producing their own computer-generated wedding invitation: a transposed snapshot of their backyard onto vellum, with the following printed message, "Please join us in celebrating our marriage. Come dressed in shades of white as we are gathering on the lawns of our home." The couple spent hours hand-decorating the borders of the invitation with a special heart-shaped rubber stamp and silver pen doodles.

Guests RSVP'd with a burst of reciprocal creativity. "We started getting a barrage of enthusiastic responses and that was half the fun," Samantha recalled, "People decorated their return post cards with their own stamps, funny sayings, cutout pictures, and photographs." Invitees even wrote clever personal messages with their regrets. It was just the kind of inventive involvement Samantha and Craig were trying to spark. Guests weren't just going to attend their wedding; they were going to actively participate!

Requesting that each guest wear white touched off another flurry of excitement. "To start out with, everyone was a coconspirator," Craig remembered. "They had to wear white just to get in!" People telephoned, sent faxes, and conversations ensued: Where do I find white? Can I wear white cowboy boots? Does it count if I wear beige?

Because the "white idea" was such a hit, for a fleeting few days Samantha and Craig entertained the notion of having all-white food. Fortunately, the idea was short-lived. Instead, they chose a caterer who prepared Southwestern cuisine that was as colorful as it was tasty: star-shaped tortilla chips, salsas in nearly every hue of the rainbow, meatless tamales, and an exotic array of other vegetarian dishes.

The decision to serve a complete meal rather than hors d'oeuvres only was a costly choice, because it also involved renting tables, chairs, linens, cutlery, dishes, and such—and hiring a full complement of service people. But the advantage was that a sit-down lunch would encourage guests to make a whole afternoon of it. So the bride and groom put conviviality first and cut costs in other areas. Less expensive champagne and wine were poured. And they reluctantly deleted the wandering, sleight-of-hand magician from their list of entertainers.

Although the couple wanted to keep their budget "realistic," their first priority was to give their creativity full rein. Samantha paid for the entire affair simply because she had more income. Her psychotherapy practice was well established, whereas Craig's was just getting off the ground. Who-paid-for-what was a nonissue between them.

Once they had settled on the caterer and menu, Samantha and Craig set their artistic sights on the wedding decorations. They split the tasks according to who wanted to do what. Conventional flower arrangements were unnecessary in the lush garden, so Craig designed something much more innovative: voice-activated sculptured centerpieces for each of the twelve tables. A mere whisper set the foot-high replicas of the bride and groom spinning, streamers and all. Samantha fashioned the wedding favors—long strands of white faux pearls for each guest to wear, individually wrapped. Each package included handfuls of glitter for tossing.

"Existential fortune cookies" became their next collective project. With the help of friends, the couple culled hundreds of inspirational aphorisms. Such sayings as "Kisses are far better than wisdom" (e. e. cummings) and "Who's not busy being born is busy dying" (Bob Dylan) were stuffed inside regular fortune cookies. One guest spontaneously became the "fortune woman," offering them to everyone from a big wicker basket.

As the Nupital Event evolved artistically, the bride and

groom began to look for "appropriate attire." Samantha started with a wide-brimmed straw hat that she absolutely adored. Her thought was to work the rest of her ensemble around it. But unfortunately, the shopping experience was far more unpleasant than she had anticipated.

> *I went through the bridal shops real fast. They made me*
> *nauseous, instantaneously. The salespeople are*
> *artificial and formal in a way that has nothing to do*
> *with me. Their first sentence right off is, "We'd like to*
> *show you some lovely gowns." And right off, I know I*
> *don't want a "lovely gown" because I want something*
> *that is not a usual wedding dress.*

Fed up with being treated like the "blushing bride" and unable to find what she wanted, Samantha took matters into her own hands, or, more correctly, put them into the hands of a seamstress. Together they designed a long white Chinese-inspired tunic that suited her taste for the exotic. Craig, too, was determined to beat the rented black-tux syndrome. He found a perfect white Italian silk suit in an uptown haberdashery. Of course, he added his own special touches—a tiger-eye bolo tie and gold snakeskin shoes!

Finding an officiant was the couple's next challenge. Several concerns influenced their choice. Neither is affiliated religiously, so asking a clergyperson to orchestrate their marriage vows would have been tantamount to asking for "input from a stranger." Furthermore, although both are spiritually oriented, neither felt compelled to make mention of God in the ceremony.

The two ended up asking a minister of the Universal Life Church, someone they had seen conducting a friend's wedding ceremony. Without the least bit of resistance, the minister readily agreed to the couple's terms: that the ceremony be conducted exactly as Samantha and Craig had written it and that they have final say over the officiant's remarks as well.

Even though the couple maintained 100 percent control

over the planning process, they still had to deflect pressure from those who insisted that they have their wedding "the right way." In casual conversation, people would say, "Of course you're going to do this . . . ," and Samantha and Craig would answer, "No, we aren't going to do that . . ." The insistent outsider would blithely reply, "But, of course, you are." Annoying "suggestions" such as these were skillfully, but politely, ignored; Samantha and Craig held firm to their vision.

But in certain areas the couple opted for the "conventional." When the time came to decide on a gift registry, Craig was more interested than Samantha. If it had been up to her, she would have written "no gifts" on the invitation. But the idea of gifts appealed to Craig, who was marrying for the first time. He visited a large department store and found a set of plates that he liked. Five friends pooled their money and bought the newlyweds a full twelve-piece place setting—the tamest, and perhaps the most practical, wedding gift they received compared to the rain stick from the Amazon jungle or the newlywed-portrait T-shirts!

In deciding to exchange wedding rings, the unconventional pair also gave in to tradition—but not without adding their own imprimatur. Initially, neither intended to wear one. For Samantha, a wedding ring had negative connotations, "not unlike calling myself a 'wife.' " For Craig, who wasn't accustomed to wearing jewelry, it was much more a matter of "getting used to the idea." He had even considered buying a gold pocket watch to commemorate the occasion instead. But ultimately, the couple feared that not exchanging rings was too much of a break from tradition, and they might be sorry if they didn't. "Having a ring is so much a part of getting married that I thought I would rather resolve my ambivalence by getting one and not wearing it, than not getting one at all," Samantha recalled. Craig felt much the same way.

Their solution: transform the rings into more than just ritual tokens. Samantha and Craig consulted a sympathetic jewelry maker and all three became involved in the design process. Thenceforth, the rings became an artistic expression. The collaboration produced companion gold wedding bands, etched with imprints of the moon, stars, and sun—perfect symbols of Samantha and Craig's profound respect for the cosmos and imbued with personal meaning.

After a year of planning, Samantha and Craig's wedding day finally arrived. Crossing the threshold of the house was like entering a magical world. The air shook with the thundering rhythmic pulse of five live Japanese Taiko drummers dressed in full native garb. Guests passed through a "virtual reality room," generated by an interactive computer program hooked up to a big-screen TV. As they congregated in the garden, they resembled a cluster of white doves against the deep green of the glade.

A hand-painted backdrop depicting oversized billowy clouds was tucked into a corner of the yard. Stepladders and chairs, arranged behind the ethereal set, invited guests to pose themselves for the photographer, instead of the routine table-by-table shots. In addition, three unmanned strategically placed video cameras ran continuously, so as not to interfere with the natural flow of the reception.

The wedding processional began to the strains of Andean flute music played by a Quechua Indian musician from Peru. Guests were gathered in the garden below as the wedding party appeared on the patio above. The bride and groom's parents, sisters and brothers and their respective spouses, and Samantha's two sons and their girlfriends wound their way down the gravel path and seated themselves in a section set apart from the standing guests.

Then came the moment when Samantha and Craig appeared, each alone, at opposite ends of the V-shaped walkway. The two met at the apex and stood hand-in-hand facing the minister. Samantha didn't want to rank friends on the basis of maid of honor or bridesmaid, so she chose not to have any attendants at all. "We are adults and we wanted to give ourselves away," said Samantha, who carried a single rose instead of a bouquet.

The wedding ceremony was brief. The minister's remarks

were succinct and spiritually inspired by references to the cosmos. Next came Samantha and Craig's self-written vows, which emphasized the values of autonomy and mutuality in their new marriage, values based heavily on Carl Whitaker's *Midnight Musings of a Family Therapist* (New York: W. W. Norton, 1989). Samantha elaborated:

> *It was important to me not to make promises or to predict*
> *the future but to make intentions and commitments.*
> *Things like "tolerating our differences" seemed more*
> *real than "I'm going to accept everything." We avoided*
> *using words like "forever," but focused on what was honest*
> *for the moment and nothing more than that.*

Wedding rings were exchanged. Then, not unexpectedly, the couple added their own inimitable twists. Instead of asking if there was anyone opposed to the marriage, Samantha and Craig said, "All in favor of this union say 'Aye.' " The guests clapped, hooted, and screamed in a burst of affirmation. As soon as the exuberant cheering died down—and it took a while—the minister said, "I pronounce you wife and husband and husband and wife"—"Just to balance things out!" Samantha added wryly.

The newlyweds kissed. The minister spontaneously turned to the guests and announced, "Ladies and gentlemen, I present to you the newest duet in town, those zany members of the fabulous Nupitones!" Hand-in-hand they descended into the garden. The Nupitones, Samantha and Craig's band, began playing "I Want to Marry You," a song written by Craig. The couple climbed onto the stage and sang together for the first time as newlyweds. And not surprisingly, their harmony was perfect!

Tips from Samantha and Craig

1. Don't be afraid of your imagination . . . let it run wild!
   Sit down and give vent to your craziest fantasies. Your
   first list should include every idea, no matter how unrealistic. Once it's down on paper, draw your inspiration
   from what you've dreamed up and then decide what is
   in the realm of "doability."

2. Use the element of surprise. Resist the urge to tell everyone in advance what you have planned. Let uncertainty
   and the unknown feed your guests' anticipation and excitement.

3. Don't throw the "bride out with the bouquet"! Just because you are planning something out of the ordinary,
   keep the time-honored wedding touches that mean
   something to you. Give yourself the freedom to be traditional if you want to be.

4. If you schedule unusual music groups who aren't used
   to playing at weddings, make sure you get explicit written agreements concerning the number of musicians
   you expect to perform, if they are wearing costumes,
   and how long or how many musical numbers they are
   obliged to play.

5. If you're dealing, as we were, with foreign musicians,
   language barriers can present a problem. Send them
   written directions to the wedding site. A week before
   confirm both the play date and time. In the same conversation, review the written directions and make sure
   they understand them.

6. If you have hired caterers, save money by buying your
   own platters or punch bowls that you'll be able to use
   in your own kitchen long after the wedding day. Rentals
   of such items are extremely costly and afterward you
   have nothing to show for it.

7. The last stage before a wedding is so stressful that you might find yourself coming apart. Consider getting counseling so you can handle the difficulties evoked by the wedding process.

8. Delegate tasks according to what each of you likes to do most. If disagreements arise, agree to table the decision until later. Return with a clear head, after both of you have had time to think about a compromise.

1950s Sock Hop Ceremony: Anne and Don

The Bride:	Age 48, second marriage
The Groom:	Age 54, first marriage
Ceremony:	Nondenominational
Site:	Friends' backyard
Guests:	125
Cost:	$2,000

Although they weren't engaged at the time, Anne and Don's wedding plans began on New Year's Eve. That night, the couple had joined a group of friends at a local "Oldies but Goodies" Club to ring in the New Year. All evening the group had sat around the table joking, laughing, and boisterously singing along to the songs they'd grown up with. Anne was sparking to the music when suddenly Don experienced an Epiphany. Then and there he proposed, exclaiming, "This is it! This is the way we oughta get married!" Four months later they did—in a musical wedding based on a medley of '50s pop love classics.

For three years Anne and Don had been living together with the fuzzy intention of marrying in the future. As soon as they nailed down a theme that excited them, they began planning their nuptials in earnest. From a practical standpoint, the couple aimed for simplicity and economy. The last thing either wanted was an "all-consuming wedding where you get lost in the process and forget about what you're doing that day." And besides, they couldn't afford an elaborate celebration.

Neither considered a conventional wedding. Anne had been married once before; a traditional affair simply didn't appeal to her. But Don had other reasons. He felt slightly self-conscious about marrying for the first time at age 54. And the thought of taking on the customary role of groom seemed "too dull—too flat." As a professional musician and singer, his tastes were geared toward a more soulful celebration. "I always imagined having Count Basie play at my wedding," Don teased. "So when he died, I decided there was no reason for me to get married!"

Fortunately, rediscovering "Oldies but Goodies" convinced Don otherwise. The '50s tunes had struck just the right chord! "Oldies evoke a time when romanticism was still alive and kicking," Don reflected. "I was in my teens then and for me, it was a decade of innocence where people felt safe and trusted each other." Anne shared Don's enthusiasm and fondness for the era. Moreover, the idea of a musical ceremony that transcended mere words appealed to her.

*We ended up writing our own wedding ceremony because
there wasn't any one particular faith or religion or
practice that covered everything we wanted to express.
It had more of a spiritual bent, more than just the standard
love, honor, and obey type thing. We wrote out what we
wanted to say and then put the whole thing to song.*

Music has the unique power to instantly link the past to the present. We all have certain melodies and lyrics that trigger nostalgic memories and longings—slow dancing, the color of a sunset, the touch of a lover's skin—and Anne and Don are no exception. The bride and groom hoped that the wedding medley would encourage married guests to renew their vows while they were taking theirs.

Shortly after the two agreed on their wedding theme, another piece of the wedding puzzle fell into place: the ideal wedding site. Wanting to avoid "a bland, cold church ceremony," the couple jumped at their friends' offer to have the wedding in their pastoral backyard, far outside the city limits. They agreed to a date, scarcely six weeks away.

Anne and Don shifted into high gear and divided the planning tasks according to what each did best or preferred to do. The breakdown was simple. Don was in charge of the music-related jobs, given his expertise as a record producer. Anne, together with her matron of honor who is a "fabulous organizer," was in charge of the food and general planning. Both had once been caterers.

As nonpracticing Catholics, neither Anne nor Don were members of a church nor did they wish to join one simply for the sake of marrying in one. Besides, Don had his mind set on an unlikely officiant—an acquaintance who had been the lead singer in "The Diamonds," a '50s singing group. There was one minor snag, however—the preferred candidate wasn't authorized to conduct marriages. The intrepid groom quickly remedied this temporary obstacle.

I ordained my own minister! I sent away $60 for the minister's license and enrolled him in a national nondenominational religious organization, which is all perfectly legal. Ironically, his parents were missionaries in China during the '30s. He came from a long legacy of religious people, so we weren't too far off base.

With the help of a graphic-artist friend, Don then designed the wedding invitation. He hunted down the original '50's sheet music for the song entitled, "Goin' to the Chapel and I'm Gonna Get Married," and used it as the background for the printed message: "Anne and Don invite you to share in the celebration of their wedding vows." At the bottom they specified " '50s Attire Optional." Don's best man took care of all the printing costs as his wedding gift to the couple.

Don, Anne, and the musical minister carefully reviewed and auditioned scores of '50s tunes, making sure that each song's lyrics added to the musical narrative of the ceremony. The songs were spliced into a standard matrimonial text that Anne and Don changed to suit themselves. Their objective to compose a ceremony that no one had ever heard before was taking shape. Once the songs were selected, Don suggested that they sing their vows as well. But Anne vetoed the idea, knowing she'd be far too nervous to carry a tune, let alone remember the words.

Finding a group of capable performers who could play well together on the first try was a snap. With years of contacts in the music business at his disposal, Don contracted top-notch musicians for the most momentous gig of his life!

I didn't just want a band; I wanted my friends to participate in our wedding and not just be observers. So I put together a handpicked group, plus some guys who'd done some harmonies together. Between them they've sold about 30 million records. Along with the songs we had selected, some of the musicians sang their own choice. We created the whole thing.

Don's wedding attire was inspired by the song "A White Sport Coat and a Pink Carnation." It took one trip to the thrift store to find everything he needed: a white tux jacket, a pair of black chino pants, a pair of spiffy spats, and a pink shirt, another gift from a friend.

Anne briefly considered '50s apparel, but then decided on a more contemporary style. Instead of looking like "a magazine bride," she chose to wear an ivory-colored cocktail dress. "I love wearing it," she told us. "Every time I put it on I have that special feeling again."

One by one the wedding details clicked into place, with little, if any, tension. The only argument that occurred between the newlyweds-to-be involved the gifts. Don wanted to specify "no-gifts" on the invitation, but since Anne had done that for her first marriage, she objected. This marriage seemed more "for real" than her first and somehow, receiving gifts symbolized an investment in the future of their relationship. Don understood. Without the least bit of self-consciousness about their age or previous marital status, the couple signed up at a bridal registry. Neither regretted it.

Just prior to the wedding, Anne's best girlfriend hosted a traditional "all-ladies," "lingerie-only" bridal shower that made up for the one Anne never had. Because Don's best man neglected to organize a stag party, Don threw himself one that was "low-keyed—jokes, music, but no strippers."

The morning of the wedding was bursting with the freshness that only an April day can bring. Don and Anne arrived early and were delighted to find the meadow-garden of the house strewn with wedding decorations, compliments of the owner's niece. Last-minute cooking preparations had proved to be "humongous" so Anne quickly called in another service person to help the one she had already hired. Although everything was prepared, hot trays needed to be arranged, garnished, and set out. Anne barely had time to finish up before getting herself ready for the ceremony.

Instead of buckling under the pressure, Anne's life experience helped her deal with all the last-minute hassles. Having orchestrated her first wedding more than ten years prior gave her a much-needed perspective on this one.

I didn't spend a lot of time worrying, I just did it. I knew if I had nine-tenths of it covered the rest would fall into place. So my attitude was, "I've done what I can, whatever happens I'll be okay with it. Let's have a good time." The cake was there, the food was there, and the people were going to show up. There's no way I could have felt that relaxed had I not gone through that other wedding. No way!

By early afternoon, a 1955 red Chevy was parked in the large circular driveway of the house, as guests began to arrive

decked out in poodle skirts with petticoats, saddle shoes, let-
terman jackets, penny loafers, and bowling shirts. Nearly everyone had gotten into the "Oldies but Goodies" spirit!

Even though they were dressed for the part, no one knew
quite what to expect. The minister, who was wearing a black
tux with black patent leather cowboy boots, took the micro-
phone and welcomed the guests. Then, he struck up the band
and sang "Why Do Fools Fall in Love," followed by that Everly
Brothers classic "Let It Be Me." Don made his entrance with "A
White Sport Coat and a Pink Carnation."

Two songs later, "Little Darlin' " began to play. As Don recited the spoken bridge—"My darlin', I need you with all my
heart and soul . . . please take my hand," Anne walked down
the garden path and joined him in front of the minister. The
unforgettable Sam Cooke song, "You Send Me" completed the
musical procession.

The minister asked the bride and groom to clasp hands as
he spoke of the passion and courage that love requires. Just as
Anne and Don had predicted, several married couples joined
them to renew their vows.

*There was no phony-pseudo reverence. It was like festival
seating—everyone standing around mingling casually.
There were no pews, no barriers. Several married
couples spontaneously joined hands and stepped forward
to be included in the ceremony. No one had ever seen
anything like it.*

When the minister concluded the marriage vows with a stirring baritone a cappella version of "Devoted to You," there
wasn't a dry eye in the house!

Anne and Don exchanged rings, promised to love and support each other, and sealed their pledge with a kiss. Without
skipping a beat, the band struck up "Let the Good Times Roll"
and the rock 'n' roll reception began!

The old saying, "God respects you when you work, but loves
you when you sing," is true—something happens to the spirit

when we raise our voices in song. Anne and Don's entire wedding became their song, a loving composition of the couple's musical memories of "then" played to the heartstrings of "now."

Tips from Anne and Don

1. When you are choosing a particular idea or theme for your wedding with an emphasis on creating something unique, think about what's most meaningful to the two of you and what might symbolize the romantic spark that unites you as a couple.

2. Make sure to allow enough time for your festivities. Our wedding was scheduled to last four hours and was too short. We regretted having to leave when we did. Many of the guests were having such a good time dancing and singing that they didn't want to leave either.

3. Great music and musicians deserve reliable, high-quality sound equipment. Set up with enough time to do a thorough sound check. Recheck everything just before the wedding. Also, measure out the dance floor with your total number of guests in mind. There is nothing worse than seeing guests itching to dance with no place to do it.

4. A bride shouldn't have to direct traffic and get married at the same time. If you are doing the wedding yourself, have someone oversee the ongoing details once the wedding has begun. That person can cue the service people to serve the cake or let you know when it's time to throw the garter so that you don't have to keep track.

5. Invite children to the wedding. Their uninhibited joy and wonder is infectious and helps adults loosen up.

6. For outdoor events, make sure your photographer knows the position of the sun in relation to the position of the altar and the scheduled time of your ceremony. You don't want to take your vows squinting into the light or be caught in the shadows.

Avowedly Creative

The beauty of creative weddings is how revealing they are. Like all creative acts, they are a kind of snapshot of the creator's unique awareness—tangible expressions of what we think, who we are, and how we feel about the world. When we collaborate with our husband- or wife-to-be, these revelations multiply and enlarge us as individuals and as a couple.

Because each person brings a different creative style to the mix, the other must listen, learn, and adapt if the team is to function smoothly. A couple must agree not to censor each other's ideas; understanding another's suggestions benefits from open questioning and unbiased assessment. With this free flow you may suddenly find yourself with a cornucopia of ideas—more than you know what to do with! And, you may even discover a new way to communicate and cooperate with your chosen one.

Other mysterious things happen when you and your mate brainstorm in the planning of your own wedding. Each partner's strengths, resistances, irritations, and aesthetic preferences will surface. As you toss ideas back and forth and they begin to take shape, you'll notice your "couple synergy" at work—a creative pulse that is greater and more dynamic than the simple sum of your separate imaginations. This exponential zap amplifies the creative energy between you, making it possible to conjure up a wedding that isn't necessarily like anything either one would have visualized individually.

Creativity blooms in an atmosphere of playfulness, love, patience, curiosity, courage, and enthusiasm. A creative wedding team must risk together, learn from mistakes, tolerate frustration, and negotiate limits. They must be able to thrive on the give and take—and love each other in spite of it and because of it! This passion, above all, breathes life into the creative process and brings ideas to their fruition. How fortunate are those passionate brides and grooms whose very relationship animates creativity, wonder . . . and a wonderful wedding!

CHAPTER 6

Remarrying with Children

Almost half of all marriages involve at least one remarrying partner. But for those brides and grooms who are already parents and want to include their children from previous marriages in their ceremony or celebration, there are no appropriate customs from which to draw. So today's couples are creating their own.

As you begin considering how to incorporate your kids into your wedding, remember that remarrying with children is neither an aberration nor an entirely new phenomenon. In fact, our very first first lady, Martha Washington, was a widow with two small children when she married George in 1759. And if the artist who captured the event for posterity was accurate, she wore a very virginal white wedding gown with a veil. So much for the etiquette naysayers who counsel second-time brides to tone down their bridal attire!

For soon-to-be-wed parents, wardrobe concerns take a backseat to a host of deeper issues, the foremost being how their children will adapt to the new marriage. Since most children whose parents remarry are children of divorce, they've probably had quite a tough time making that life-changing adjustment. In fact, recent studies reveal that children will most likely feel the effects of their parents' divorce well into adulthood. Dr. Judith Wallerstein studied 131 children of divorce from 60 middle-class families over a period of fifteen years; here are some of her conclusions:

> Children navigate through divorce and later enter new families with a greater sense of anxiety and apprehensiveness about the reliability of human relationships. They bring to the new families a sense of having been aggrieved, of having lost out on a first and critical step ... All children suffer from divorce, no matter how many of their friends have gone through it. And although the stigma of divorce has been enormously reduced in recent years, the pain that each child feels is not assuaged. Each and every child cries out, "Why me?" [*Second Chances: Men, Women and Children a Decade after Divorce*, Judith S. Wallerstein and Sandra Blakeslee. New York: Ticknor & Fields, 1989, pp. 233, 303.]

Because of the inevitable emotional trauma associated with divorce, it is important that mothers and fathers embarking on a new marriage be sensitive to their children's ambivalence about yet another transition. You may be utterly ecstatic over your newfound love and the opportunity to begin life afresh, but such a transformation means something quite different for your child. He or she may fear that a new spouse will encroach on their territory, deprive them of your love and attention, upset the status quo of single parent and child "together against the world." Additionally, a new stepparent whose role will be similar to that of the child's real parent may trigger fears about conflicting allegiance.

The ages of the children involved and your family's unique circumstances will dictate how each situation should be handled. Probably the most crucial thing to remember as you approach this new chapter in your lives is to talk with your children, listen to them with an open mind, and try to understand what they're feeling.

Before you begin to plan your wedding—and before you tell anyone else—inform your children of your decision to marry. They should be the first to know. And tell them without your husband- or wife-to-be present. That way, your children will be more free to express their true feelings. Emotions buried in an effort to please future stepparents are likely to surface later and be more difficult to deal with. Communicate your own happiness but also acknowledge that the new marriage will be an adjustment for everyone concerned. Assure your child that the family will work together toward making that change as easy as possible. It's also important to let young children know, if such is the case, that a stepparent will not take the place of their birth parent. Nor will stepsisters or stepbrothers in any way deprive them of your love.

Once you've announced the news and your children have aired their concerns, try to involve them in the excitement of planning the wedding. Obviously, the ages of the children will determine how they might participate. A young child could visit the church or wedding site with their dad or help their mom decide on favorite flowers. A teenage son or daughter may want to record tapes for the reception or accompany you to the studio to select a photographer. Offspring of any age would probably love to sample wedding cakes as you comparison shop together. No matter how old your children are, it's important to take your cues from them. Suggest jobs or activities that coincide with their interests, but don't force them to do anything.

Conversely, don't give children too much control either. Young children will feel overwhelmed if you burden them with too many choices, and it's inappropriate to allow even older children to make final decisions. After all, it's your wedding, and even though your children may play an important part in it, make it clear that veto power rests with you. When you take your daughter or son with you to the florist or bakery, ask for their opinions, but give them a limited range from which to choose, making sure either choice meets your approval. For instance, "Which do you like better, the raspberry-layered Madeleine cake or the anisette with almond?"

If at all possible, and using the preceding guidelines, allow your children to have some input into their own wedding attire. This should be one of the most enjoyable parts of the wedding. Boys and girls alike, especially younger ones, usually adore the chance to dress up in "fancy" clothes. Whether your child is going to be your flower girl or junior bridesmaid, ring bearer or best man—or simply walk down the aisle as part of the processional—they'll take pride in looking their best. Give them the opportunity to be part of the whole process of picking and choosing.

One novel idea for younger children is to let them dress like the bride and groom. Eileen and Ken from Chapter 2 asked Ken's mother to make a miniature wedding dress for Eileen's six-year-old daughter, Jennifer, who is absolutely thrilled about being flower girl. Her five-year-old cousin will be the ring bearer, dressed in a mini-tux to match Ken's. "They're going to march down the aisle looking exactly like me and Ken," Eileen told us. "It was Ken's idea, and Jennifer loved it. It gave her an even more important role in all of this and made her feel more connected to the ceremony."

Jennifer's delight at being such an integral part of the festivities is due in part to Ken and Eileen's openness with her from the beginning. Six months into their relationship, Jennifer asked her mom if she was going to marry Ken. Eileen sensed Jennifer's uncertainty about Ken's role versus her daddy's, and mother and daughter talked about it at length. Ken and Eileen prepared Jennifer for their marriage step-by-step by respecting her concerns and assuring her they would be met with honest, straightforward answers. For example, they explained what role Ken would have in disciplining her and what role her own father would retain. Being an only child himself, Ken was also very sensitive to Jennifer's fears about having to share her mom with someone else. He has ultimately been able to win Jennifer's trust by demonstrating to her that "gaining" a stepfather doesn't in any way mean "losing" her mommy.

How your children are included in the wedding will depend not only on their ages but on their relationship with your fiancé and how they feel about your getting married. They can join in the prewedding planning by

- Accompanying you on visits to the florist, photography studio, bridal salon/tuxedo shop, bakery, caterer, and such
- Helping you keep track of RSVPs
- Figuring out seating arrangements at the kids' table
- Discussing the kids' menu
- Making special cards or gifts for guests at the rehearsal dinner

They can participate in the wedding service by

- Signing in guests at the guest book table
- Ushering guests to their seats
- Passing out ceremonial programs
- Being a member of the bridal party
- Joining with you in a ceremony celebrating the creation of a new family (some parents even give children special rings or medallions to "wed them together" as a family)
- Reciting a special prayer or poem

Additionally, there are a number of ways to make children feel important by involving them in the reception, such as

- Greeting guests in the receiving line
- Offering a special toast
- Acting as master or mistress of ceremonies for a designated period of time
- Helping to serve the wedding cake
- Passing out packets of rice or birdseed
- Getting together with the other kids at the wedding to make a special crayon-colored oversized greeting card for the bride and groom
- Tying tin cans and spraying "Just Married" onto the getaway car with shaving cream

The bottom line is that you want your children to feel included in the celebration and to have fun. The parents and children in the stories that follow came up with their own ideas—some wild, some tame—about how to achieve these twin goals. We think you'll be inspired.

A Family Picnic: Heidi and Bruce

The Bride:	Age 28, second marriage; 4-year-old son from previous marriage
The Groom:	Age 29, first marriage
Ceremony:	Methodist
Site:	Park
Guests:	75
Cost:	$5,000

Heidi:
Anyone who happened to stroll by the park at that moment might have had a hard time figuring out just what kind of party it was. There I was in my very Victorian wedding dress seated next to Serafina-the-Clown, who was tossing out wrapped party favors to a crowd of noisy four-year-olds!

Bruce:
Fortunately, I love children, so having all the kid-oriented stuff at our wedding was great. There were a few raised eyebrows on the part of some of our childless friends, but all in all having the kids there lent an added dimension!

When Heidi announced to her four-year-old son, Nathan, that she and Bruce planned to be married, he giggled and began dancing around to the familiar chant, "Mommy and Bruce sitting in a tree, k-i-s-s-i-n-g . . ." Neither surprised nor up- set, Nathan was excited by the news. Bruce had been part of his life for about a year and a half, and the two had had a chance to develop a close relationship. Nathan's biological fa- ther moved out when Nathan was 18 months old and remar- ried when the child was two, so Nathan was used to having two separate households with two different father figures. Now the only problem was containing all that excitement and an- ticipation; the wedding was still three whole months away, an eternity in the life of a four-year-old!

One of the first decisions Bruce and Heidi made was to somehow create a "party within a party" for Nathan's play- mates. Their reasoning was twofold. First of all, most of their closest friends were parents of the kids at Nathan's day-care center, so it seemed natural to invite their children. Second, they wanted to let Nathan share the day with his own pals. By having his own "wedding party," he would not only feel impor- tant and intuit the significance of the day, he would also have a great time.

But in order to even consider having a kids' party as part of their celebration, Bruce and Heidi had to agree that an in- formal wedding was indeed what they both wanted. Like Char- lotte and David from Chapter 3, and other second-time marriers with whom we spoke, Heidi's first wedding had been a very formal affair, so this time she was certain she wanted something much more casual. But she was concerned that Bruce have the kind of wedding he truly wanted as well. This is what Bruce had to say:

> *I've been accused of being too easygoing, and Heidi asked me point blank, this being my first—and only—marriage, did I have my heart set on a church wedding and a fancy sit-down dinner? She should have known better. Formality has never been my thing, and I was happy to have the excuse to have it outdoors in a more laid- back atmosphere.*

Heidi added with a laugh:

Inviting fifteen preschoolers definitely headed off any threat of formality. And Bruce is about the most unpretentious person I know, but I just wanted to make sure he wouldn't come to me when we were sixty-five and regret that we didn't have a traditional wedding like everybody else's.

Since they were planning a June wedding, Bruce and Heidi thought the park at a nearby lake would be perfect. It was both a beautiful setting for a wedding—with lots of picnic tables and shady weeping willows—*and* a great place for the kids to run around and play. With plenty of jungle gyms, monkey bars, and ducks to feed, there was little chance the children would be bored while their parents partied. Still, factoring in that "little chance," Heidi went one step further. She thumbed through the classifieds in the local *Parents Only* newspaper and found the names of entertainers for children's birthday parties. It was actually Nathan who made the final choice; it seems Serafina had officiated at a recent birthday party and was a big hit. She brought cool party favors, tied balloons into many different animal shapes, and painted everyone's face so you couldn't even recognize them.

Serafina would entertain the kids for about an hour. But Heidi wanted to make certain that parents would be able to enjoy the entire wedding without worrying about supervising their preschoolers, so she also hired two teenage girls from the neighborhood to oversee the kids for the entire afternoon.

Because nearly a fourth of the wedding guests would be Nathan's friends, Bruce and Heidi thought it would be appropriate to include his name on the wedding invitation. The invitations thus became a family project. A friend of Bruce's owned a photography studio that specialized in "old time" sepia portraits, complete with turn-of-the century costumes and antique props. Dressed in Victorian finery, Heidi, Bruce, and

Nathan had their portrait taken and used it as the basis for the wedding invitation, which read, "Heidi, Bruce, and Nathan request the pleasure of your company at the wedding of Heidi and Bruce. Lakeside Park, June twelfth at eleven a.m. Family picnic to follow . . ."

The old-fashioned portrait was apropos. Heidi planned to wear an off-white Victorian lace wedding dress, and Bruce got his friend at the studio to lend him and Nathan nineteenth-century-style tuxes. "I liked the idea of dressing up in clothes from a different era," Bruce said with a grin. "It took the edge off the overly serious tone weddings sometimes have. Heidi and I both wanted this to be a fun time."

In keeping with the theme of a bygone era, the couple found a caterer who agreed to make up family picnic baskets—similar to the ones their great-grandparents probably enjoyed on Sunday picnics in the park. Each basket would contain enough fried chicken, biscuits, fruit salad, and cole-slaw for a family of four. (Special "salads and biscuits only" baskets were prepared for vegetarians.) In addition to the tra-ditional wedding cake, there would also be a dessert buffet, complete with children's favorites such as chocolate-chip cookies, brownies, and ice cream cones (a specialty of the kid-friendly caterer!). Champagne and fruit punch rounded out the menu. The caterer would be responsible for setting the picnic tables on the morning of the wedding; supplying table-cloths, napkins, plates, and utensils; and bringing simple daisy-filled vases for each table.

Only a few more details remained. With just three months' notice and June being the most popular wedding month, the minister at Heidi and Bruce's church was unavailable on the Saturday they needed him. Disappointed but undaunted, Heidi contacted the university chaplain at the nearby college she had attended almost ten years ago. He not only remem-bered Heidi but was honored that she wanted him to officiate at her wedding. The couple met with him and explained that, in addition to the traditional Methodist service, they also wished to write their own vows. The minister had no problem with that or with performing the ceremony in the park, and keeping it brief for the sake of the children.

Although they wanted Nathan to be an integral part of the wedding festivities, Heidi and Bruce were both very clear about why they thought it inappropriate to include him in the actual ceremony. Heidi explained:

> The wedding ceremony itself is about Bruce and me joining as husband and wife. As much as Nathan is affected by our vows, they're not his vows to take. I know other people feel differently about this, and I've heard of ceremonies where the children exchange rings and so forth, but that wouldn't have felt right to me. I'm Nathan's mother and I will love him and take care of him no matter what. And Bruce is his stepfather and has certain responsibilities toward him. But what exists between Bruce and me is something distinct.

Bruce talked about needing to preserve the essential meaning of a wedding ceremony:

> I had absolutely no problem inviting all Nathan's friends, including him on our invitation, or having a clown at our wedding. But that didn't change the fact that a wedding is to unite a man and a woman in matrimony. To have had Nathan in the ceremony really would have felt strange to me, so it wasn't anything we even considered.

Heidi did, however, want Nathan and her father to walk her down the aisle. Like many remarrying brides, she came up against some dogmatic attitudes from so-called authorities.

> I had read in several etiquette books that it's not really proper to have your father give you away if you've been married before. But my dad had recently come through a serious operation, and it meant a lot to me

*to have him walk with me. I didn't look at it in terms
of him or Nathan "giving me away." It was just that, other
than Bruce, they're the most important men in my life.*

Not everyone feels the same about including their children
in the wedding processional or ceremony. Samantha, from
Chapter 5, said it would have seemed "weird" for her grown
sons to escort her down the aisle. She and Craig walked down
by themselves as a symbol of their maturity and independence. What's important is that you be your own judge of
what seems most appropriate.

Once they'd resolved the how-to-find-a-minister-in-June dilemma, Heidi and Bruce's only other planning problem cen-
tered around the question of music. Both of them, but
especially Bruce, were set on having live music for the reception. "I was in a band in college, and I've always considered
myself a musician at heart," Bruce confessed, "so the thought
of having taped music was a real turnoff." But the park
wouldn't allow amplified music of any kind, so a rock band
was definitely out. They were about to give in to a silent celebration when a friend told them about a "string quartet" he'd
heard recently at another wedding. "A string quartet?" Bruce
winced, his rock sensibilities slightly offended. But it turned
out the group actually billed itself as a "swing quartet," a vio-
lin, stand-up bass, and two acoustic guitars. They played an
eclectic mix of jazz, rock, and pop with a 1940s swing style.
Heidi and Bruce went to hear them at a local club, loved their
music, and hired them for both the processional/recessional
and the reception. (The Parks and Recreation Department
said unamplified strings were no problem.)

Nathan was up at 6:30 A.M. on the day of the wedding, much
too excited even to watch Saturday cartoons. Four-and-a-half
hours later, looking very handsome in his vintage tux, he
walked down the aisle with his mom and his grampa while
the swing quartet played some music called "Pachelbel's
Canon", which Nathan liked to call "Taco Bell's Cannon." He
sat between his grandparents and watched as the minister pro-

nounced his mom and Bruce "husband and wife." Nathan thought it was funny when they kissed in front of everybody.

He and his friends took off for the playground right after the ceremony. While the grown-ups hugged and drank champagne, the kids played on the swings and the slides, and ran back up the hill to see if lunch was ready. Grown-ups always take a long time to eat, but Nathan and his pals finished quickly so they could go play hide-and-seek near the jungle gym. Serafina the Clown couldn't find them at first. But when she announced that she had party favors for anyone who was interested, fifteen squealing youngsters followed her. Nathan's mom came over and helped pass out the brightly colored "squish balls" before she was called back to cut the three-story cake with the tiny bride and groom on the top. Nathan and his friends made faces at each other after they'd had them painted like cats and monsters and Ninja Turtles.

A little later, Nathan was finishing his second ice-cream cone when the music stopped and his mom called him over to dance with her. Everybody was watching and Nathan felt embarrassed at first, but pretty soon all his friends got up and danced with their own mom or dad.

When it was almost time for his mother and Bruce to leave on their honeymoon, Nathan became a little sad. Even though his grandma and grampa were going to take him to the zoo and the movies and the museum while his mom was gone, he wasn't going to get to go to someplace called "Alaska" with his mom and Bruce. He cried a little while his grandma held him in her lap. Then she reminded him of his special job. Secretly she showed Nathan where the tiny packets of birdseed were hidden in a basket under the tree. He passed them out to all his friends and told them to get ready to throw it when he said so. Bruce and his mom looked real happy as they waved to him from their car. Nathan's grampa held his hand and asked him if he knew what a honeymoon was. Nathan just rolled his eyes.

Tips from Heidi and Bruce

1. If you decide to have lots of young children at your reception, make sure you have fun things for them to do, a space large enough and separate enough so that they don't completely take over the adult party, and someone to supervise.

2. Consider hiring a special children's party entertainer. They know how to keep large groups of little ones amused for at least an hour, and their fee is usually fairly reasonable.

3. If you don't want to hire an entertainer, think about paying an experienced baby-sitter or child-care worker to not only keep an eye on young children but plan a few activities as well.

4. Make sure to inform your childless guests that there will be children at the wedding. At least then they'll be forewarned.

5. Schedule your "bring the kids" wedding for early in the day. Toward late afternoon and evening even the sweetest little creatures can become tired and cranky.

6. Be sure to designate a close friend or relative to oversee your child during the wedding. Ideally, that person will also be the one your son or daughter will stay with while you're on your honeymoon.

7. Don't even think about coming back from your honeymoon without kid souvenirs!

We All Said "I Do": Deborah and Greg

The Bride:	Age 39, second marriage; son age 12, daughter age 11, son age 6, from previous marriage
The Groom:	Age 40, third marriage; son age 12, son age 9, daughter age 8, from previous marriages
Ceremony:	Civil
Site:	Restaurant
Guests:	150
Cost:	$10,000

Deborah:
We wanted the wedding to symbolize that we were blending two families into one. What was most important to us was incorporating the six of them into the ceremony as much as we could.

Greg:
It was very complicated with all the kids and everything. Keeping it all together. It was a big step, a big change.

As soon as Deborah and Greg started dating, there were the inevitable quips comparing them and their progeny to The Brady Bunch. Actually the friends and family who so labeled them weren't very far off base. With Greg's three children from two previous marriages and Deborah's three from her one, the couple did indeed have the same number of combined offspring as their TV counterparts. Like that most famous blended family, Deborah and Greg's children ranged in age from six to preteen. But unlike the TV show, Greg and Deborah's story centers on the months leading up to the day when their families became The Russell Bunch.

Not long after their romance began, Greg and Deborah made a conscious effort to plan joint outings with their two sets of kids. Both are devoted parents who hoped that their children could learn to enjoy one another's company. The eight of them went to parks, restaurants, and movies together—and were soon spending weekends as a group. Greg's comfortable house was usually the scene of these gatherings. Fortunately, the children got along relatively well, owing, in part, to their closeness in age.

But each child had his or her own issues regarding the formation of this new family. Greg's son from his first marriage was the only one who had real difficulty adjusting to his future stepsiblings. Because he lived with his mother most of the time, he wasn't around for many of the group activities, and often felt like an outsider when he visited his dad. Also, having spent little time with his half brother and sister, he had grown up essentially as an only child. Now he had to get used to an additional three kids who weren't even biologically related to him.

Greg's other two children saw their mother rarely, because Greg had sole custody of them, and they seemed to appreciate and enjoy Deborah's company. Conversely, Deborah's children maintained close ties to their real father, who had been divorced from their mom only about six months when Greg and Deborah started dating. Their problem wasn't so much the idea of new stepbrothers and stepsisters as coming to terms with the recent divorce.

All six children had nearly a year to get used to the idea that Deborah and Greg were a couple before Greg proposed.

Deborah:
  At that point I'd already asked my kids how they felt about my dating Greg. We'd talked things over quite a bit. So when he surprised me with an engagement ring, they kind of knew it was coming.

Greg:
*When I told my children that I had asked Deborah
to marry me, they were all very excited. The two
younger ones were especially thrilled to be getting a new
mom.*

Deborah's 11-year-old daughter, Nicole, was actually the first child to hear the news. Perceiving her to be the most mature of the six kids, Greg took her into his confidence and showed her the ring about two weeks before giving it to Deborah. It became their secret. Nicole felt especially privileged to know about the plans that would ultimately join the two families.

While Nicole happily welcomed the event, Deborah's six-year-old son, Jordan, had a different reaction. "My little boy was more protective of me," Deborah recalled. Knowing that boys of Jordan's age are more defensive about their single moms, Greg let Deborah be the one to announce the engagement to him and to her twelve-year-old son, Eric. But there was another reason why Jordan was particularly apprehensive about his mom's new marriage and why Greg and Deborah were sensitive to his feelings. A few months earlier, Jordan had attended his father's wedding and came home sobbing, telling Deborah, "This was the worst day of my life." At that time, only about a year had elapsed since Deborah had divorced her first husband, and Jordan was just beginning to realize that his dad and mom weren't going to get back together. Unlike his older brother and sister, Jordan was openly miserable as he watched his father marry another woman.

By the time Deborah and Greg announced their wedding plans, Jordan had had an additional six months to adjust to his parents' divorce as well as nearly a year of adapting to his future stepfather and stepsiblings during their weekly outings and get-togethers. Still, with Jordan's negative experience foremost in her mind, Deborah vowed to make her wedding a positive experience both for him and the other children. She desperately wanted them to enjoy the day and share some of the happiness she and Greg felt.

Deborah and Greg first set about planning their ceremony, a principal part of which would symbolically welcome all the children into their new family. Raised as a Catholic, Deborah would have liked to have been married in the Catholic Church. But due to the Church's proscription forbidding divorce, that was impossible. Fortunately, a friend referred the couple to a judge who took a personal interest in their upcoming marriage ceremony, especially when Deborah and Greg told him they wanted to write a special part of the ceremony that would join together their two families. The judge thought it was a wonderful idea.

The theme of "family" also figured prominently in the wording for their invitations, which was deliberately inclusive and didn't focus only on the bride and groom. On the outside of the soft mauve invitation was an oval window cut out to reveal two embossed roses; it was inscribed "And the two shall become as one." Inside, it read: "We have experienced love . . . in our parents, our families and friends, and now a new love in each other. With sincere joy and a firm desire to give this love its fullest expression, Deborah and Gregory invite you to share in their happiness as they exchange marriage vows . . ."

Unlike some other second-time brides, Deborah wanted a big wedding. She had eloped when she was nineteen and felt cheated out of the wedding she always dreamed of. "When I didn't have that—the gown, the veil, the whole thing—I was very crushed. It was always a big regret of mine." So this time Deborah decided she would have as large a gathering of friends and family as she could, even though Greg would have preferred a more intimate affair. But he knew how important a proper wedding was to Deborah and wanted her to have one.

Still, there were those who couldn't resist giving the couple unsolicited advice, "You should do something smaller. Why do you want to have such an elaborate wedding? It's so complicated with all these kids!" Deborah remembered feeling pressured and wondering if maybe she *was* too old to be making such a big deal out of this wedding. But she quickly came to her senses and stuck to her guns, reminding herself, "What's the difference if I'm getting married at twenty or thirty-nine? It's my day and I'm just as happy!"

Although Deborah and Greg would have preferred an unlimited guest list, there was one area where they were forced to cut back: other people's children. Because most of their friends have three or four children, there was no way they could afford to invite entire families. They made an exception in the case of the matron of honor's children, but otherwise spread the word that the wedding was for "adults only."

Figuring that it would be easier to hold the wedding and reception in the same location, they chose an elegant Italian restaurant in their neighborhood and reserved the entire establishment for a Sunday, when it was closed to the public. Together with the chef, they selected the sit-down luncheon menu, including a number of special dishes for the children. They also arranged for a separate children's table, since they knew their kids would enjoy sitting on their own.

As a thirty-nine-year-old second-time bride, Deborah agonized over what to wear. Like Heidi, she'd read "somewhere in some dumb bridal book" about the proper behavior and attire for remarrying brides. Not only were they not supposed to walk down the aisle with their fathers, they were advised not to wear a traditional white bridal gown or a long veil. After some deliberation, Deborah decided, "I'm just gonna do this!" and bought a beautiful long, white beaded dress with sheer sleeves. Preferring to look more sophisticated than the average twenty-year-old bride, she found the dress in the "gallery department," not the bridal salon, of an upscale department store. Modifying her description of the dress a few seconds after she described it to us, she added, "Well, actually, it was off-white."

Deborah was clearly nervous about doing the wrong thing and still somewhat intimidated by "the rules." She allowed herself the white/off-white dress, but much as she wanted to, couldn't bring herself to buy a veil.

*They're so beautiful, but I thought I couldn't wear one
because everything I read seemed to say I was too
old. That's something I would change if I had it to
do over. It's so silly. I've been to several weddings since
mine where the brides were my age and wore veils!*

Meanwhile, the children began their involvement in the
planning process. First by helping to choose what they would
wear and second by specifying the roles they wished to have
in the processional and ceremony. Deciding on the boys' out-
fits was easy: they'd wear tuxes just like Greg's. But serious
conflict arose concerning the girls' attire. The bottom line was
that Deborah's eleven-year-old daughter, Nicole, refused to
wear the same dress as Greg's eight-year-old daughter, Heather.
Acknowledging that this was a reasonable demand, Deborah
let each girl pick out a different style dress in a similar color
and fabric. Both girls would be dressed in peach floral prints
and wear flowers in their hair.

Then there was the question of which child would walk
down the aisle first and who would have what ceremonial
function. Not wanting to slight anyone or risk any hurt feelings, Deborah and Greg negotiated carefully. All six children
would be part of the wedding party and the family vows, but
each one would also have "their time," their moment in the
spotlight. Each would march down the aisle alone in order of
height, the shortest going first.

The "wedding job assignments" weren't as sensitive. The two
older boys, Eric and David, would be ushers; Nicole and
Heather got to carry flowers; Greg's nine-year-old son,
Brandon, was in charge of the guest book; and six-year-old Jordan would be the ringbearer. All parties seemed satisfied, with
the exception of a few minor disputes: "How come I can't
carry flowers?" Jordan wanted to know. To which his mother
answered diplomatically, "Well, because you get to carry the
ring, and that's a very special job."

The day before the wedding all the children helped decorate the house that was to become theirs as a family. The res-

taurant was reserved for the next day from 11:00 A.M. to 5:00 P.M., but about fifty guests were invited to come back to the house after the reception. Wanting the place to look festive, the children strung up yards of white crepe paper and hung white doves and wedding bells throughout the house and in the yard.

That same afternoon Deborah and Greg called them all into the living room and presented each child with a special gift: silver I. D. bracelets for the boys, a more feminine version for the girls, all with the date of the wedding engraved on the back. The couple told them that the gifts were from "their new mom and dad" in the hope that they would always remember their wedding day.

Greg took the boys to his place that evening, and Deborah had her mom come over to look after the girls. Then Deborah did something just for herself. She hired a masseuse to come to the house to give her a premarital massage. Afterward, she poured herself a glass of wine, took a long bubble bath, and luxuriated in the child-free quiet of her bedroom. "I was so tired and so stressed from all the wedding preparations. It was wonderful to have that night to myself."

The two girls got dressed with Deborah and her mother on the morning of the wedding. Even with wedding-day jitters, they all had fun getting ready in the giddy sorority atmosphere. But things weren't going as smoothly over at groom headquarters. The boys were being boys, clowning around and making it nearly impossible for Greg to get the four of them dressed. Getting them to sit still long enough to fasten four little pairs of cufflinks was too much for him, so Greg finally turned the job over to his best man. Then Jordan had a nosebleed (not an unusual occurrence) and got bloodstains all over the front of his tux. As if that wasn't enough, Greg spilled coffee all over the kitchen floor. The final aggravation occurred when he couldn't find the keys to his car! "Greg was definitely nervous that day," Deborah remembered. "If you look at him on the videotape just before the ceremony, he looks like he's about to have his thyroid removed."

Despite all the mishaps, everyone made it to the restaurant on time! The children walked down the aisle looking proud, anxious, delighted, solemn, happy, and tentative. Best man and matron of honor preceded the radiant bride who gently took the arm of her father and then joined her groom and their children at the altar. Bride and groom gave long-stemmed roses to each of their mothers seated up front. The ceremony began.

The children formed a circle around the couple, and the judge recited the following words Deborah had written:

> *Today we celebrate the marriage of Gregory and Deborah*
> *and the uniting of their children. Today David, Eric,*
> *Nicole, Brandon, Heather, and Jordan, together with*
> *their parents, strive to become a loving family, to support*
> *and love one another, and to consider themselves blessed*
> *to be part of each other. Deborah and Gregory ask*
> *God's help and guidance in raising these children—*
> *and wish them to know how much they are loved . . .*
> *Gregory and Deborah, secure in this foundation, your love*
> *signifies a relationship in which your independence*
> *is equal, your dependence is mutual, and your*
> *appreciation of one another is reciprocal.*

As guests converged on the happy couple after the ceremony, Deborah and Greg, their parents, matron of honor, and best man formed a receiving line, hoping that the children would become part of it as well. But the under-thirteen members of the bridal party took off for less formal activities, including chowing down on the kid meals their parents had ordered for them. Later, though, the children made their feelings known to the roving videographer who asked each of them to say a few words for the camera. Greg's boys said they were really glad to have a mom. Heather remarked that she was happy to finally have a sister. The others wished their parents luck and gave them all their love. But, looking impishly into the camera, Jordan came up with the most inventive remark of all: "Does this mean we get an increase in our allow-ance?"

After the meal, a close friend of Greg's made a special toast to the entire eight-person clan. Then the DJ, a personal friend of Deborah's, sprung a little surprise. He spoke about how they were now one big happy family, called them all up to the dance floor, and instructed them to hold hands. Over the speakers came a rousing rendition of "The Russell Bunch," set to the tune of the original "Brady Bunch" soundtrack. Some-how, Greg and Deborah should have expected it.

Tips from Deborah and Greg

1. Make the children feel special by giving them a partic-ular job. Try to draw them into the excitement of plan-ning the wedding by talking over various details beforehand.

2. If a child says they *don't* want to do something, listen to their concerns and try to work out a solution they'll feel more comfortable with.

3. Go with your heart. Even if your parents or friends ad-vise you to "scale down" a second or third wedding, do what makes you and your children happy.

4. Get the word out to your guests about an unusual wed-ding gift we received: gift certificates for family-style res-taurants. With so many children, eating out together is a treat we rarely indulge in!

5. Registering is an especially good idea for remarriers, because friends who are uncertain about what you already have and what you still need won't have to guess.

6. Try to make arrangements for someone to take care of your kids the night before the wedding ... and treat yourself to an at-home massage!

Remarrying with Teenagers or Adult Children

The preceding wedding stories have dealt primarily with the concerns of parents with younger children. Although parents of teenagers will tell you that those between the ages of thirteen and nineteen are in a category by themselves, some of the same wedding advice applies. Ask them how they feel about your remarriage; listen to what they have to say and accept any ambivalence they might have; let them know you'd like them to be part of your wedding in some way; and, finally, take your cue from them. Remember that teenagers may have a more difficult time both expressing what they're feeling and accepting a new stepparent. Dr. Judith Wallerstein explains it this way:

> *The adolescent is engaged in one of the central tasks*
> *of growing up—separating from the adults in his family*
> *and beginning to carve out a separate identity. The*
> *teenager inevitably challenges adult authority, which*
> *becomes embodied in the stepfather who has just entered*
> *the scene. As the internal drama of the adolescent*
> *is worked out on the family stage, the stepfather—*
> *through no fault of his own—becomes an antagonist or*
> *perhaps even a villain, just by virtue of being there.* [Second
> Chances, p. 248]

This does not mean that every bride or groom with a new teenage stepson or stepdaughter should prepare themselves for emotional battle. Every family's dynamic is different, every person is different, and your teenager's response to the new marriage will depend largely on the kind of relationship they have with both birth parents. But even if your teenager or stepchild is delighted and relieved that their parent has found a mate, be prepared for their resistance to a new person having authority over them.

Be creative when including adolescents in your wedding; target their interests and ask for their input, but don't be pushy. If your seventeen-year-old daughter is a fledgling filmmaker, ask if she'd be willing to video the ceremony or reception. Is she into fashion? Take her with you to shop for your dress and treat her to a special lunch afterward for being your fashion consultant. A fifteen-year-old boy with a green thumb might help you spruce up the backyard for your at-home wedding. Or if he's the outgoing type, maybe he'd agree to make the opening toast at your reception. Teenage children can also serve as ushers, best men, or junior bridesmaids.

Once your children are grown and on their own, their relationship to you naturally takes on a different slant. With independent lives of their own, they will probably feel less threatened by your remarriage than teenagers might. Still, other issues arise. Adult children may feel protective of you and concerned about your making the right choice. And their idea of the right choice could be vastly different from your own. If a middle-aged mother decides to marry a younger man, her twenty-seven-year-old son might be very concerned about such a union. And even when the new stepparent seems an appropriate match, there is always the inevitable comparison with the real parent. Or, as with several remarriers with whom we spoke, your grown children might act like overbearing parents, dictating what is and what isn't an appropriate wedding in your circumstances. Perhaps they think it's in poor taste for a couple in their 40s or 50s to have a lavish wedding, complete with sit-down dinner and a five-piece band. If this happens, you'll have to treat them as you would anyone else who would try to take over your day: tell them politely to back off.

If you're lucky, your adult children will be as happy for you as you would be for them were they about to embark on a new life with the person they loved. And, like David's son, they will honestly wish you well. David, from Chapter 3, enjoys a close relationship with his 28-year-old son, Jason, and the two speak quite openly with each other. When David imparted the news to Jason, the young man was glad that his dad was marrying Charlotte. It seemed only natural for Jason to accept his father's relationship, since David and Charlotte had been friends for so many years. Jason had only one bit of sage advice for the father he cared about so deeply, "Dad, don't screw this one up."

Ten Tips for Remarrying with Children

1. Be sensitive to your child's possible ambivalence about your remarriage. Listen to their concerns and assure them that your love for them is constant regardless of the changes that are taking place.

2. Involve your children in wedding preparations and give them a special role in the ceremony or at the reception, but consider their age and their interests. Never force them to do anything they don't want to do.

3. If you're incorporating children into your ceremony, be sure to discuss your agenda with the officiant. Plan on enough time to rehearse with your kids so they'll feel confident the day of the ceremony.

4. Be flexible. Weddings with children may not be as predictable as weddings without, but they have their own special delights. If an eight-year-old stepson will be crushed unless you allow him to be "assistant best man," or if a six-year-old daughter insists on being

ringbearer, consider whether their hurt feelings are worth adhering to protocol.

5. Offer to let each child invite at least one friend. It will make them feel more a part of the festivities.

6. Try to have older preteens and teenagers sit with their peers at the reception. They'll be insulted if they have to sit at a "kids only" table with five-year-olds!

7. Don't forget to provide special kid food for younger children. Beef Bourguignon or spicy blackened chicken won't cut it with the younger set. Let your kids help plan the menu.

8. Give your children disposable cameras and let them document the day from their point of view.

9. If your child is having a problem with some aspect of the wedding and nothing seems to soothe him, think about underlying causes and talk it over. The difficulty may stem from his inability to accept the new marriage.

10. For information regarding stepparenting, contact: The Stepfamily Association of America, 215 Centennial Mall South, Suite 212, Lincoln, NE 68508-1834; 402-477-7837. They can put you in touch with local groups holding meetings in your area. Also ask about their quarterly publication "Stepfamily Bulletin" and other educational materials.

CHAPTER 7

~

Leaving Town to Tie the Knot

Weddings have always been one of the more delightful excuses to travel. Who is traveling where is changing, however. Because we all seem to be scattered to the winds, questions arise as to where a wedding should be held. In many cases, the bride and groom stay put and weddings are planned locally. Friends or members of the couple's extended families who live elsewhere—out-of-town, out-of-state, or even out of the country—travel to them.

But in our mobile society, this problem isn't always so easily solved, and brides and grooms find all sorts of good reasons to leave town to tie the knot. A bride and groom may simply want to stage this extraordinary moment in their lives in an equally extraordinary setting, far removed from their normal environment. Or a long-distance site may be chosen because the spouses-to-be shared a romantic interlude there. Then again, because it is increasingly rare for the bride and groom to share the same birthplace, let alone to have remained in their hometowns into adulthood, they may decide to have their wedding "back home" where most members of one of their families live. And sometimes just the opposite is true: getting away for the wedding is a tactic for escaping family and the tension and pressure that often accompany them.

Political summits, conventions, and family reunions are all

planned long distance—so why not weddings? After all, we live in a shrinking world, a global village where transcontinental or international travel no longer takes days, but hours. Improved communications have made a tremendous difference in our ability to plan an event and make instant decision making possible. Faxes, overnight mail, modems, and teleconferencing obliterate time zones as if we were in the same room with a hotelier or florist. The result is that "far away" doesn't always seem so anymore.

But wait. Mention that you are planning an out-of-town wedding and some people will roll their eyes, try to talk you out of it, or begin to raise your doubts. Your luggage containing the irreplaceable wedding gown might get lost on your way from Minneapolis to Miami. Your friends who can't afford the time or the money to travel that distance are going to feel left out. And all the presents—it will cost a fortune to ship them home UPS.

Aren't weddings complicated enough without adding the inconvenience of distance? As you will see in this chapter, the answer to this important planning question is yes—and no.

Naturally, no two long-distance weddings are alike. But several controlling factors influence the ease or difficulty of the planning process, including (1) how elaborate your wedding plans are, (2) the creative liberties you want to take, (3) how far you live from your wedding location, and (4) how exotic or remote your wedding site is. What follows is logical: simple, traditional, long-distance weddings are the easiest; elaborate, creative, long-distance weddings are more challenging. Leaving town to tie the knot usually takes an extra measure of effort, more patience, and a higher tolerance for less control. In a strange way, planning a long-distance wedding has much in common with marriage itself!

Caribbean Ceremony, Reggae Reception: Amy and Doug

The Bride:	Age 22, first marriage
The Groom:	Age 41, first marriage
Ceremony:	Civil ceremony
Site #1:	Hotel garden—Nassau, Bahamas
Guests:	2
Site #2:	Hotel reception—Seattle, Washington
Guests:	130
Cost (for either):	$12,000

Be honest. Haven't you, at least once, considered escaping with your fiancé and leaving the wedding mania far behind? What if you could wake up and forget all the irritating details that are left undone? No more harpist auditions. No more dickering with the hotel over the cost of liquor service. No more Mom reminding you that pale peach gives your skin a green cast and that ecru is better.

What if you could just elope?

Although the idea of elopement crosses most of our minds, relatively few of us choose to do it. Whether this is because elopement is tainted by old-fashioned notions of illicit love or that actually going through with it might disappoint too many people (including ourselves) is hard to say. But what if there were a way to have the liberated feeling of "running away" *and* the euphoria of celebrating with family and friends?

Amy and Doug found a means to have both by cleverly crafting a modified elopement: a Caribbean ceremony for just the two of them combined with a reggae reception back in the States, attended by all their friends and family. For Doug, an inveterate traveler, this plan was the next-best alternative to marrying "on a raft floating down the Ganges." The image of taking his vows on a secluded coral cay satisfied his adventuring, irreverent nature and his romantic leanings for a private wedding moment with Amy.

Amy was motivated to divide her wedding ceremony and celebration for more practical reasons. To begin with, her parents weren't enthusiastic about Doug, who is twenty years their daughter's senior, and did not wholeheartedly support her decision to marry. Resistance or none, Doug and Amy had every intention of becoming husband and wife. By planning the ceremony in a distant location, the newlyweds-to-be offered Amy's parents the option of attending or the excuse not to. Just to be fair, Doug gave the same choice to his mom and dad, knowing they wouldn't travel that far.

> We didn't want the family stuff that goes on around weddings
> to happen while we were actually getting married.
> That's what we tried to circumvent by going away.
> Also, we wanted a wedding for us! The ceremony itself
> wasn't as important as the fact that we were out in the
> world together, exploring by ourselves.

Not ones to miss the best excuse to throw a great party, the couple decided to schedule their reggae reception immediately upon their return from the Bahamas. By then, any objections would be moot; Any and Doug's marriage would be a fait accompli. "We were not into 'Let's make this an eternal moment,' " Doug explained. So the idea of having a typical wedding reception scarcely entered their minds. Instead, they pictured a honeymoon homecoming—a weekend affair held in a major Seattle hotel where guests would stay for two nights and "party." The plan made perfect sense for several reasons. Because they and all of their out-of-town guests would be flying into Seattle International Airport, it was easier to remain in Seattle than to drive another two hours to Yakima, where the couple live. Also, in Amy and Doug's view, a large metropolitan hotel could accommodate all of their traveling guests as well as provide full service for the special needs of their event.

Amy took the lead, organizing the reception long-distance from Yakima with the objective of having everything set up prior to leaving for their Caribbean ceremony. Over a period of five months, she made several overnight trips to Seattle to meet with the hotel events planner. What she didn't accomplish in person, she faxed or discussed over the telephone. The planner was happy to recommend vendors—everyone from the photographer to florist to a designer who was hired to transform the hotel ballroom into a tropical paradise for the night of the reggae reception.

Amy was particularly keen on serving Caribbean-inspired cuisine to her wedding guests, but anticipated resistance from the hotel kitchen staff. Much to her surprise, convincing the chefs to experiment was far easier than she expected.

We met with the hotel cooking staff beforehand and brought a Caribbean cookbook along. They got really excited because it gave them a chance to do something different for a change. We went through the recipes together and picked out dishes that were realistic. It wasn't totally authentic, but it was close enough.

There wasn't anything from the regular catering menu—not even a standard wedding cake. Instead, we had fried bananas and ice cream for dessert!

While working closely with the hotel personnel saved time and worry, Amy didn't accept every suggestion the planner made, especially since Doug was paying for everything. Once the hotel realized that they were dealing with a couple who had their own concept, they backed off on the usual wedding add-ons. Amy described how they kept an eye on their budget.

We kept a close tab on the cost per person; Doug is a building contractor so he bargains for everything. The hotel was pushing for an open bar, but we decided to cover only beer and wine—the guests had to buy their own hard liquor.

Doug also insisted that the designer give us some unit costs on the decorations. At first, the guy seemed to have the attitude, "This is your wedding and you're probably willing to spend any amount here." He wanted to charge us two hundred dollars for a stuffed monkey! But once Doug started pinning him down item by item, we were able to cut the costs by a quarter.

Not only was the couple in tight control of their costs, they took strict inventory of their guest list to guarantee they'd be spending their marathon wedding celebration with those they genuinely like and rarely see. Doug drew the line and stuck to it.

My age has a lot to do with the kind of wedding I had because I am less self-conscious about what I am doing and less afraid of offending people. Take the guest list, for example. My mom gave me about seventy-five names and I crossed out every one I didn't know or like— that was about 50 percent of them. Amy was the same way. She just invited people that she was in contact with or liked and that was it.

Access to a large hotel took the hassle out of making room reservations for the expected out-of-towners. Not only could everyone stay in one place, they could do so at reduced rates. The couple negotiated a special price for a block of sixty rooms. To make the booking even easier, a self-addressed hotel reservation card was enclosed with each wedding invitation. Guests could choose to stay at the hotel where the newlyweds' extended celebration was scheduled or make reservations elsewhere for as many or few nights as they wished.

Amy and Doug's quasi-package approach to planning their reception suited their overall attitude toward their wedding reception. "The best part of doing our marriage this way was that we didn't work ourselves up for months ahead of time about 'The Wedding,' " Amy told us. "It was more like, 'We're going on this vacation and we're getting married.' "

If the couple had a motto to guide them throughout the course of their planning, it would have been: "Make it nice, but make it easy!" Because they had freed themselves from the anxiety that often accompanies a traditional wedding affair, they felt entirely comfortable handing over the administrative details to the hotel staff. The best part was that once the major decisions were made, Amy and Doug were able to devote themselves to their real passion: the romance of traveling together.

It was Doug who made the arrangements for their Caribbean ceremony. He had visited the Bahamas before and was familiar with the area. A few weeks prior to their departure he called the Bahamas Tourist Bureau's Wedding Service to organize the necessary paperwork. In addition to completing certain documents, officials told him that a minimum four-day stay was required before they could marry. This stipulation was hardly an inconvenience, because the couple planned to island-hop for ten days anyway. All they had to do was pack their bags, head for Seattle's International Airport, and fly to the pearly turquoise of the Caribbean! Apart from preparing for the day of the ceremony, the rest of the trip would be impromptu—no reservations, no itinerary—a beachcomber's dream.

The couple arrived in the Bahamas on a jewel-like day. They checked into the Gray Cliff Hotel, a hundred-year-old colonial mansion renowned to have the best wine cellar in the Caribbean and located in the heart of Nassau. It took no time at all for the hotel staff to reserve the garden for the ceremony, order the flower arrangements, hire a photographer, and arrange a meeting with the magistrate who would administer the vows. Amy entrusted her full-length white wedding gown to the concierge for pressing. And that was it—every detail done in *one* day!

The next morning, Amy and Doug left for their prewedding

honeymoon to visit half a dozen secluded islands. Ten days later, on a Wednesday, they returned to Nassau to find the Goombai Music Festival in full swing. Throngs of reggae fans filled the streets and a carnival spirit swept the city on the day of their wedding!

About an hour before their ceremony, Amy and Doug were sipping champagne and nuzzling in the hotel pool without a care in the world. The couple was so nonchalant that they even forgot to make dinner reservations! Amy described their brief, but intimate, vows in the luxuriant garden of the hotel.

> We weren't concerned about the ceremony being "perfect." My father and sister flew in for the day and we invited this old guy who was the blues piano player at the hotel, too.
>
> The ceremony was over in about ten minutes. We said something personal to each other at the beginning and then the magistrate read the vows. Then we went over to the Goombai Festival and wandered around, me in my wedding dress and Doug in his tux. Everyone else was in shorts!

Within the next twenty-four hours, the newlyweds flew back to Seattle, picked up their car at the airport, and checked into the hotel where their reggae reception was to be held.

Tan, relaxed, and still on island-time, Amy and Doug weren't prepared to hear or deal with the slipups that awaited them: the "honeymoon suite" with twin beds, the lost room reservations, the mix-up in rates, and the no-show airport shuttle for their arriving guests. "I think if we had designated someone to troubleshoot while we were away, it would have been better," Amy said. "That way the problems wouldn't have hit us all at once." The newlyweds' abrupt reentry began with several "intense discussions" with the hotel manager, after which the irritating oversights were sorted out.

Apart from these last-minute annoyances, their reggae reception, the weekend's centerpiece, unfolded flawlessly.

Guests were treated to a sensory taste of the tropics—bouquets of birds of paradise, mock palm and banana trees, booths with thatched roofs, and a fanciful menagerie of fake monkeys and parrots! Each hut featured an array of Nassau rum punches—including the infamous "Goombai Smash"—and tray after tray of exotic West Indies cuisine.

And, of course, there was the rousing reggae band, a local group from Yakima that the couple had heard many times. At first, the older guests requested standards like "Misty" and "New York, New York." Here, the band was out of their depth and stuck close to their tried-and-true repertoire with tunes like Bob Marley's "One Love." Finally the infectious beat caught on and, by the end of the evening, the whole party was dancing. To add to the festivities, the couple hired a caricaturist and a bartender who doubled as a comic and a juggler!

Yet amid the Island theme-party atmosphere and revelry, certain traditional wedding accents were given their due. Amy wore her full-length white wedding gown and Doug his black tux. The newlyweds danced a "first dance" (even though it was to a "hot" reggae song). And there were rounds of laudatory toasts in honor of the bride and groom.

Amy and Doug's freewheeling spirit shone through every aspect of their wedding—from its inception to the final sip of the last Goombai Smash! Doug summed it up best when he said, "You can plan and plan and plan for a perfect wedding, but the one thing you can't plan for is romance." And, fortunately for these newlyweds, romance is one thing they don't seem to be running short on.

Tips from Amy and Doug

1. Arranging a wedding in a foreign country can be complicated. It's easiest to select a host country whose language you understand and speak.

2. Marriage requirements differ from country to country. Check with the appropriate local consulate or embassy in Washington, D.C., for specific marriage requirements.

3. Contacting all the proper authorities and organizing the legal paperwork for the host country often takes more time than you might think. In addition, you may need to take special medical tests or have certain records translated to complete their nuptial requirements.

4. Find a local contact in the host country to make sure you've fulfilled all the stipulations or to help you resolve a problem after you've arrived. A designated authority or an attorney are your best bets.

5. Remember: If you don't satisfy a host country's rules, they won't let you get married. Don't expect them to make an exception for you!

6. Don't forget, just because you have been legally married in another country, doesn't mean you are legally married in the United States. If you are interested in a legally binding marriage here, you must complete the requirements of your state as well.

7. Planning problems crop up continuously. If you plan to be absent up until the very last minute before your reception, designate a troubleshooter who will oversee and reconfirm details pertaining to the plans you've made.

Bicoastal Nuptials: Judy and Abel

The Bride: Age 23, first marriage
The Groom: Age 30, first marriage
Ceremony: Protestant

Site:	The United Nations Chapel (ceremony)/Chinese restaurant (reception)
Guests:	300
Cost:	$35,000

Planning a large-scale wedding from afar requires time, persistence, and a certain amount of blind faith! Fortunately, Judy and Abel had all three when they decided to marry in New York, three thousand miles from southern California where Abel attends law school and Judy works as an assistant editor at a local publishing company. So while neither the bride nor the groom was in a position to pay for a large wedding themselves, they were responsible for planning one. "The hardest thing about having a long-distance wedding is trusting someone else to follow through and make decisions," Judy said, thinking back. "I wish we could have done it ourselves, but there was no way we could have."

Because Judy and Abel each have different hometowns, choosing the city where their wedding would take place was a complicated decision, one that was influenced by their parents' interests as well as their own. Judy, a Chinese-American, was born and raised in New York City, where the majority of her friends and large, tight-knit family live. Abel is a Los Angeles-born Colombian. His mother and immediate family live in L.A. also, but most of his extended family, including his estranged father, still reside in Colombia. Abel has no family on the East Coast and few were expected to attend from Latin America.

Because this was Judy's first marriage, her parents were eager to host a ten-course Chinese wedding banquet for their extended family, numerous business associates, and many old friends. Since their guests outnumbered Abel's family's nearly seven to one, they were set on having the wedding in New York.

However, Abel's mother would have preferred to have had

the wedding in Los Angeles. She offered to underwrite the affair on the condition that it be held there, figuring that the expense of covering her guests' air fares to New York would be roughly the same as the costs of a West Coast wedding. But Judy's family balked at this idea. Not only would a greater number of their guests be forced to travel, but the traditional role of the bride's mother would be significantly diminished.

After several tense parental negotiations by phone, and one tearful, face-to-face confrontation in a Los Angeles deli between the couple and their respective mothers, a solution was arrived upon. In the interest of economy and harmony, the New York location won out. Judy's parents would host the Chinese banquet and Abel's mother would contribute five thousand dollars toward the general wedding fund. In addition, she would host a Los Angeles reception a month or so after the one in New York for West Coast friends and relatives who were unable to attend the New York wedding.

Relieved that this decision was behind them, Judy and Abel surged ahead. Planning a local wedding is hard enough, but planning one in another city can easily turn into a logistical nightmare. Researching suitable vendors; interviewing prospective florists, caterers, and musicians; and comparing prices are time-consuming activities even when they are local, let alone on the other side of the country.

Knowing this, the couple extended their initial one-year engagement to two years, assuming the extra prep time would compensate for the extra mileage. Needed, too, was an "on-site point person" to gather referrals and follow up on the hundreds of details that tend to get lost in the greater sweep of events. Judy's mother was poised for action—the willing and obvious choice.

Right from the beginning, Judy and Abel worked closely with Judy's mother and kept in constant contact, mostly by phone. For all their major decisions, the couple scheduled quick trips to New York. Because of Abel's class schedule and Judy's job commitments, these junkets were squeezed into weekends or during holidays. Judy and Abel became experts on travel bargains, including discounted fares, frequent-flyer deals, and red-eyes. From Day One of planning to the day of their wedding, they traveled back and forth five times.

Judy and Abel's first three-day planning mission to New York took place two years in advance of their actual wedding date. The couple arrived with a lengthy checklist and a tight schedule within which to accomplish everything. But what the couple didn't count on was that formal introductions to Judy's extensive family came first. "The first trip in August we got absolutely nothing done," Judy recalled. "It seems like all we did was drive here and there so that Abel could meet my family, which is huge." Their overly ambitious agenda was forced to take second place.

What little time was left over that weekend was spent evaluating two possible locations for their wedding. First, Judy's mother suggested her church. The newlyweds-to-be felt it didn't quite suit them, and Judy's grandmother came to their rescue. She objected on the grounds that it was facing a cemetery. "You don't want dead people looking at you while you are getting married," Grandma protested!

The couple also rejected the second site, Judy's parents' country club. Beautiful, but way too expensive, even at discounted member prices. Sunday came and very little had been accomplished, but at least the social preliminaries were out of the way. The couple returned to Los Angeles eager to get down to the nitty-gritty and looking forward to their next trip.

Over Thanksgiving break, Judy and Abel returned to New York a second time to focus on two specific tasks: finding a church (it had to be air-conditioned for their June ceremony) and a Chinese restaurant that would accommodate three hundred guests. Accomplishing both objectives over the long weekend proved to be a great deal more challenging than the couple had expected.

Although Judy and Abel were both baptized Catholic, Abel has also been affiliated with both Mormonism and Judaism over the years. Unless Abel was willing to get a special dispensation from the Catholic priest, marrying in a Catholic church was out of the question. As he was unwilling to invest the time or long-distance effort to do so, the couple narrowed their site search to Protestant churches.

For one full day, the couple literally "ran" in and out of churches, which were, for the most part, "too small and too stuffy." Frustrated and tired, the couple was about to shelve their quest when Judy's aunt suggested the United Nations Chapel, where she herself had gotten married. The chapel proved to be the perfect solution: spacious, nondenominational, an international roster of officiants to choose from, inexpensive and, as it turned out, close to the restaurant where the couple ultimately held their reception.

With the chapel chosen, the couple turned their attention to finding a suitable restaurant for their traditional Chinese wedding banquet. The stakes on this decision were high, given that time was of the essence. Judy and Abel didn't know when they'd be returning to New York again and were aware that the restaurants there are often booked years in advance. With two days left of their stay, the pressure was on.

Judy's mom had gathered suggestions beforehand, so with recommendations in hand, the couple hit the streets of Manhattan. Even though Chinatown is honeycombed with restaurants, nothing appealed to them. Either the ceilings were too low, or the rooms were too dark, or the service was too slipshod. Scores of establishments later, the possibilities were looking grim. Abel described how their luck changed at the very last moment.

None of the restaurants seemed right. Finally, we saw this nontraditional-looking Chinese restaurant right across from Radio City Music Hall. We couldn't even taste the food because you have to be wearing a tie just to be seated. It didn't matter. We walked into the place and fell in love with it.

The airy, split-level space looked more like an avant-garde art gallery than a restaurant. Jazz played softly in the background. Light streamed into the dining room through the enormous picture windows. Once the newlyweds-to-be saw the restaurant's menu and a photo portfolio of weddings that had taken place there, their minds were made up. But Judy's parents preferred a more traditional ambience and weren't so easily persuaded. After all, they were footing the banquet bill and were concerned that the food meet the highest standards. Judy and Abel boarded the plane without convincing them, and doubting if they could.

Judy's parents and grandparents, former Chinese restaurateurs in their own right, prepared to make a tough appraisal. A few weeks later, they skeptically sampled the nouvelle Chinese cuisine. After a delectable meal, Judy's parents were still wavering. They had two minor objections concerning the absence of Chinese waiters and the lack of round tables that, for Chinese, symbolize unity. But Judy's grandmother minimized these concerns and mustered her generational clout to win their seal of approval. That night Judy's father put down a deposit for the banquet dinner. With a deep sigh of relief and many thanks to Judy's grandmother, the couple checked off one more major item on their list.

It wasn't until visit number three in March that the couple actually tasted the restaurant's food for themselves. Every dish they ordered was superb. But this trip wasn't about enjoying the culinary delights of New York. It was about interviewing photographers, auditioning bands, and making final decisions about both—again, all in the course of one weekend. While in Los Angeles, Judy had made judicious use of her East Coast contacts and set up back-to-back appointments with prospective candidates.

I used to work for a paper in Staten Island, and I had a friend who was dating an action photographer. I called him from L.A. and he recommended someone else. Then, I called the second photographer, spoke with him extensively over the phone and made an appointment

to see his portfolio when we arrived in New York on
Friday.
    I also knew some local photographers that my family
had used in the past who had cheap package deals. Their
quality couldn't compare with the guy I had found through
my girlfriend. Getting married is a once-in-a-lifetime
thing and there is no do-over. So we decided it would
be better to spend the extra money and get it right.

Finding a good band was infinitely more complicated. The
couple was content with simply hiring a DJ, but Judy's parents
insisted on having live musicians and lined up three leads, to
be auditioned Saturday and Sunday. This took some doing
since each band was playing in distant locations from Judy's
home on Staten Island. Those two days were a blur, with
nearly seven hours on the road and seven hours of listening
to music. Abel shuddered as he remembered how dreadful
the first audition was.

We drove two hours to see the first group. And that was
a complete waste of precious time. The band was
playing at a VA hospital in New Jersey. The leader
was like a game-show host from the sixties. Bad—really
bad. No one in the audience was even listening.

Saturday was nearly gone by the time the exhausted couple
returned to Staten Island. Later that evening, they "crashed" a
stranger's wedding to see the next group. Standing in the
wings of a large ballroom Judy and Abel eavesdropped on the
band's performance. At first band members wore ties and
jackets and were taking ten-minute breaks. But as the evening
wore on, the musicians looked woefully bedraggled—ties cast
off and shirttails hanging out—and their breaks extended to
nearly a half-hour.
    Judy and Abel woke up worried on the morning of their
Sunday departure. They packed and fretfully left for the airport. On the way, they made one final detour to Long Island

where the third band had an office. It was about an hour from
Judy's house and in the opposite direction from the airport.
There they screened an entire videotape of a wedding for
which the group had performed. They were impressed, but
still had reservations.

Nevertheless, the time for more auditions with more groups
was gone; Judy and Abel had to make a decision. In a matter
of hours, they'd be on a plane headed for California. If there
were ever a moment when the two felt up against the wall,
this was it. Judy described their dilemma.

> *The last band we auditioned was very professional but
> they were seven pieces and we only wanted five. They
> said they couldn't play with fewer because it would
> compromise their sound. After we had seen the other bands
> that were so bad, Abel and I felt we had no choice. So
> we went with them even though they were more
> expensive.*

If visit number three was frazzled and down-to-the-wire, visit
number four in June was just the opposite. The newlyweds-
to-be threw themselves wholeheartedly into the sweet task of
selecting the wedding cake. During three ambrosial days, the
couple did little more than bakery-hop. Judy loved every fat-
tening minute of it.

> *We had a list of pastry shops from a local New York bridal
> book. If you tell bakeries you're cake shopping, they'll
> prepare a whole tray of samples for you. So we just
> went from one to the next. We took my brother along
> for a third opinion, and the three of us sampled everything
> in sight. But be careful—don't do this just before you
> buy your wedding gown!*

A dozen bakeries later, they ordered their cannoli cream
cake filled with chocolate chips from the same Little Italy bak-

ery that had prepared Judy's parents' wedding cake twenty-five years earlier.

Preparations for the wedding party's attire began a month or so thereafter, but were complicated by the long distances. Judy selected a pattern for her bridesmaids' dresses and, through Abel's mother, found a dressmaker in Los Angeles. But since only one of Judy's five bridesmaids lives there, the four remaining out-of-town bridesmaids had to send meticulous measurements to the dressmaker and hope for the best. Once the dresses were completed, extra time had to be factored in so as not to rush the final fittings in their respective four cities: New York, Chicago, Washington, D.C., and Atlanta!

Judy's wedding attire followed Chinese tradition, which prescribes that the bride change clothes three times during the course of the wedding celebration. In order to simplify matters, Judy chose to make all of her attire arrangements in Los Angeles. Her traditional white wedding gown was made by the same Los Angeles dressmaker who sewed the bridesmaids' dresses. Judy also purchased a red silk, high-collared "Suzy Wong"-style dress in a store in Los Angeles' Chinatown, and her third change, a white going-away outfit, in a nearby department store.

Because the wedding team was so well organized, nothing else had to be done until the following spring. Abel's mother had taken care of the invitations, and Judy's mother came out to Los Angeles in mid March to help with the final details of Judy's dress and the guest list.

In April, Judy and Abel returned to New York for the fifth and last time before their June wedding. This visit was made to attend their East Coast wedding shower and to select the final floral arrangements. The bride and groom also signed with Macy's Bridal Registry in New York, which electronically cross-registers to Bullocks and I. Magnin in California. The couple had a West Coast wedding shower as well, upon their return to Los Angeles.

After scrupulous planning, Judy and Abel's wedding was ready to take place. The couple arrived in New York two weeks ahead of time to enjoy the whirlwind of prewedding get-togethers and to attend to last-minute details. When June 19 arrived, the bride and groom were well-rested, well-feted, and on top of the world. Three-thousand miles, five turn-around trips, and two years after they began planning it, their bicoastal wedding came off without a hitch.

Tips from Judy and Abel

1. Time is sanity: The farther away you live from the location of your wedding, the more time you need to plan for it.

2. Find a dedicated person(s) who will serve as liaison to follow up and follow through on wedding details. Close relatives who care about making your wedding memorable are excellent choices.

3. Don't expect to have the same degree of control as you would if you were planning your wedding locally. Know that at some point you will have to put your trust in other people's decisions.

4. If you're limited as to the number of times you can visit the wedding location:

   Network with those who live in the wedding site city, but rely only on recommendations from those whose tastes and standards you trust.

   Narrow your choices *before* you arrive. Use faxes and overnight mail to exchange information with vendors before your meetings and to confirm agreements afterward.

   Although it is sometimes unavoidable, try not to make a hasty decision just because you feel pressured for time. If you don't feel good about the vendor, don't hire them. You'll be sorry later when you're too far away to do anything about it.

5. Telephone bills can be outrageously expensive. Sign up for special low long-distance rates if you don't already have them.

6. If you don't live in the same town in which you are holding your wedding, consult the almanac for the average weather conditions around your projected wedding date. Keep temperature and humidity in mind when selecting a wedding site.

The Not-So-Great Lakes Getaway: Jayn and Jeff

The Bride:	Age 46, third marriage
The Groom:	Age 49, second marriage, 23-year-old son and 26-year-old daughter
Ceremony:	Protestant
Site:	Washington Island, Lake Michigan
Guests:	100
Cost:	$6,000

Summertime on Washington Island, Lake Michigan, Wisconsin: A white gingerbread house overlooking the lake, lazing in a hammock on the veranda, listening to the sound of the waves slapping the dock and the cicadas in the forest. A perfect location to get married. At least that is what Jeff and Jayn thought when they decided to use this remarkably romantic location for their wedding.

But this wedding-from-afar was plagued with mishaps, miscalculations, and unforeseen hurdles that were simply out of the couple's control. Much of what went wrong with Jayn and Jeff's wedding could have been predicted, knowing that not-by-the-book weddings are much more difficult to plan and execute long distance than traditional ones. For those who are thinking of planning a creative wedding in a creative location, there's a great deal to be learned from Jayn and Jeff's Not-So-Great Lakes Getaway.

"The island," as Jeff calls it, has been in his family since his grandfather acquired the property in the early 1900s. He has been going there every summer for as long as he can remember. It is where he learned to fish for bass and fell in love for the first time at age twelve. "The greenery, the woods, and the tranquil eccentric community with lots of writers and iconoclasts, appealed to me," Jayn began. "We wanted to share the island with our friends and family, most of whom live in the Midwest." And besides, Jeff added, "It's the greatest place for a three-day blowout party!"

Washington Island is as remote as it is beautiful. The small community, originally pioneered by Icelandic immigrants, is not only far away from everything, it is far from a logistical dream. Start in Milwaukee, then drive two hundred miles along the Lake Michigan coastline to Sturgeon Bay. Continue north forty-five minutes outside of Sturgeon Bay where you'll find the ferry landing. Hop the ferry and forty-five minutes later arrive at Washington Island. Unlike many other long-distance wedding sites reachable by daily direct flights, reaching the island poses a formidable challenge. A quick trip there is simply impossible.

But if there were ever a "can-do" couple, it's Jayn and Jeff. She is an information technical specialist for a major utility and he heads a Central Coast winery. Both are comfortable with planning complicated, large-scale projects; they manage them daily in their work, so why not tackle a long-distance wedding?

Since the island retreat is owned in trust by Jeff's family, the first order of "business" was to get permission to have temporary run of the property from the other shareholders: Jeff's mother, brother, cousin, and ninety-three-year-old Uncle Wilson who lives in Arizona. In January, eight months prior to their wedding date, the couple wrote letters detailing their plans to everyone, "just to clear the decks."

Uncle Wilson's go-ahead was critical, because his summer house was to be the actual site of the wedding. The "big house" has a well-equipped kitchen, spacious living room, and wraparound veranda large enough to accommodate Jayn and Jeff's one hundred guests—just in case it rained and the ceremony had to be moved inside. Within days, the couple received a unanimous and jubilant go-ahead.

With family politics taken care of, the bride and groom turned their attention to creating a wedding combining "the dignity of a major transition with a lot of spirited whimsy." And why not? With three previous marriages and two traditional weddings between them, Jeff and Jayn were ready to leave most of what wedding etiquette had to offer behind! At this stage in their lives, the couple was much more concerned that their wedding represent "a realistic picture of who we are and who we want to be." Unfortunately, their simple, straightforward vision was to transform itself into a complicated endeavor in no time.

Jayn and Jeff visualized a three-day affair with guests invited to camp on the grounds, bunk in the four houses on the property, or lodge in one of the local inns. Day 1: Settle-in, fish, play golf, boat, or simply relax in the spectacular setting and, later that evening, roast the newlyweds-to-be at a prewedding dinner. Day 2: Attend their afternoon country wedding by the lake. Day 3: Say farewells at a picnic-style brunch.

Even though Jayn had only visited the island twice, she pictured the scene of her wedding as clearly as if it were in her own backyard. A swath of lawn leading down to the water in front of the grand old Victorian house. Large serving tables draped in white antique linens with under cloths of bright-colored fabrics. Big wicker baskets spilling over with wildflowers gathered from nearby meadows. Freestanding awnings for shade—and maypoles, forty of them. "Maypoles are happy things and I thought that they would fit in with the natural environment," said Jayn. "I could just picture the ribbons fluttering in the wind next to the lake."

So convinced that their plan was doable at a distance and within their time frame, the couple decided to take a spring "pre-honeymoon" in Europe. That meant that most of the groundwork for their August 8 wedding would have to be completed by May 1, their scheduled flight date. If they returned to the United States on June 9, they'd have nearly two months to catch up at work and prepare to leave for Wisconsin by August 1. No problem!

Jayn and Jeff selected their wedding team and meticulously set up their computerized checklists. All the arrangements that only an island insider and resident could accomplish, such as lining up the entertainment, making the inn and golf reservations, contacting local vendors, and finding a wedding officiant were handled by Jeff's mother and cousin who live there year-round.

But the real linchpins of the plan were Megin, Jayn's best girlfriend of seventeen years, and Megin's husband, Tim, who live in Toledo, Ohio, a "mere" two days' drive from the island. Megin was eager to help out in any way she could and put herself on call. Tim, a professional chef, insisted on becoming Jayn and Jeff's "wedding-cook-in-residence" for three days and took charge of *every* detail, from soup to nuts.

By February, Jeff and Jayn were busy designing the maypoles—seven-foot tall wood poles with concrete bases and approximately seventy feet of streaming ribbons per pole. Jeff industriously engineered but never executed, a prototype. The first small setback came when Jayn realized forty maypoles would require almost three thousand feet of ribbon. "I soon found out that the ribbon alone would be tremendously expensive, around $2,000," Jayn said, wincing, "so Megin said she could get it cheaper in Toledo and put that on her 'to do' list."

The original plan called for the maypoles to be fully assembled in California then transported back to Wisconsin by truck. But when the couple realized the cost involved, they shifted into contingency mode. After a blizzard of long-distance calls to Wisconsin lumber mills, they finally found one that would deliver the raw poles to the island a few days before their arrival in August. Unless Jayn was willing to abandon the maypole idea, there was no getting around it: they would have to be assembled then and there.

Meanwhile, Jayn was scouring antique stores for linen tablecloths. Once the collection was large enough, she had everything washed, starched, and packed to be shipped to the island. Along with her personal china, crystal, and silver serving pieces, and cases of wine from Jeff's vineyard, there was a total of twenty-three boxes! Shipping expenses were mounting by the minute.

March and April flew by. Jayn and Jeff were heartened and relieved by Tim's impeccable follow-through. After he and Jayn planned the three-day menu over the phone, he quickly established a network of purveyors, worked out an ordering and storage agreement with one of the island grocery stores, and prepared an exhaustive list of necessary rentals— everything from steaming tables to warming trays to industrial-sized kitchenware. Scrambling to find these items proved to be complicated and very time-consuming. "Unless you know the exact size or number of an item or can point to a picture in a catalog, describing stuff like this over the phone can be a nightmare," Jeff recalled, rolling his eyes. With their characteristic persistence, however, the couple managed to find a source in Sturgeon Bay.

Jayn spent even more phone hours painstakingly reviewing all the decorations with Megin: fabric, baskets, ribbon. Megin assured Jayn that all was purchased according to her specifications and that the decorations would be delivered to Washington Island as agreed. As a backup, Jayn proposed meeting in Chicago two days earlier, but Megin couldn't make it.

The two friends, whose communications had always been "nearly telepathic," thought they were understanding each other perfectly. But, unfortunately, they had gotten their wires crossed. For when Jayn arrived on the island the Tuesday before her Saturday wedding, she discovered that the results were "gruesome."

No matter how many times we went over the decorations, there were fundamental differences in perception and taste that we couldn't have known about beforehand. We could use the same words to describe something but didn't have the same image in our minds.

So when I said colorful under cloths for the food tables, she was hearing bright and cheap. I was not sending the message. Her idea of a good buy was twenty-five yards of orange chiffon! What I should have done was gotten photographs or samples of cloth. But by the time I got to Washington Island, that mistake was unrecoverable.

Orange chiffon was to be the least of Jayn and Jeff's worries in what was quickly to become a series of logistical logjams. Megin, Tim, and their children (who were doubling as the cooking staff) arrived not only with all the party supplies, but with mounds of camping gear as well. Within a day a "tent city" sprung up on the grounds of the summer retreat. Jeff's family bristled.

Even though we had gotten permission to use the land months before, my family didn't anticipate what having that many guests meant until it was actually happening. The rules started changing. My aunt started saying things like, "Well, we don't know if you can have the wedding at the big house because your Uncle Wilson has to take a nap in the afternoon!" Suddenly, it became too much for them to bear and they began retreating and took their promises with them.

So, just when the arrangements should have been coming together, they began falling apart. Jayn was scheduled to take the ferry back to the mainland and meet Jeff, who had flown in one day later. Before she left the island, she left explicit instructions with the twenty or so family members, many of whom were teenagers, to start assembling the maypoles.

At Sturgeon Bay everything went like clockwork. The bride and groom filled out the obligatory paperwork for the wedding at the county courthouse. Jayn loaded the two rented vans "up to the gills" with the rental items. The couple ferried back to the island expecting to see progress in the maypole construction. But much to their dismay, the maypole brigade had gone on "vacation." The few poles that had been completed "looked like something from the "ragpickers ball." Jayn was infuriated. She gathered up the mangled maypoles and tossed them into the woods, only to find that they'd been resurrected the next day by those who had made them!

Other calamities followed: Uncle Wilson officially withdrew the use of his summerhouse, so that Jeff's smaller cabin became wedding headquarters. All of the party supplies were moved into the cabin's cramped kitchen equipped with little more than a primitive four-burner stove, minuscule oven, and a temperamental dishwasher. To make matters worse, the toilet went on the blink.

By Thursday, Jayn and Jeff were beside themselves, but had no other choice than to make the wedding happen anyway. "We used sheer determination and humor," Jayn said with a tense smile. But what saved the couple's sanity was their ability to separate their personal disappointment from the larger family dramas that were playing themselves out. The couple had two distinct perspectives on the family situation—both of them equally valid. As far as Jayn was concerned, Jeff's family was distinctly uncomfortable with her take-charge attitude. Throughout her stay on the island she sensed their underlying hostility.

Weddings are times of collisions and change, and that change isn't always welcomed. The conflict that is already going on in families is amplified. Jeff had been

*married for 24 years and everyone in their family had
their set role. Here I come into the picture and I'm very
different from Jeff's ex-wife—much more assertive and
independent minded. If the roles were reversed, my
family probably would have acted the same way.*

Understandably, Jeff's interpretation was different.

*The island is a place which has always been very territorial,
very private—especially for the older family members.
I think the wedding felt like an invasion to them. The
dynamics were difficult. I was caught in the middle trying
to appease everyone—Jayn and my family—and minimize
the impact of all these strangers.*

Despite the cataclysmic events, Jayn and Jeff's wedding was
beautiful. The guests assembled by the lake, which was literally shimmering in the sunshine that summer Saturday. Sail-
boats billowed by. The wedding party emerged from a path
through the woods: Jayn, in her Mary McFadden black-and-
white gown carrying a bouquet of wildflowers, and Jeff, in a
black tux. Accompanying them were Jeff's mother, his two
children, and Jayn's niece and nephew.

Standing before a local minister, Jayn and Jeff read their
vows to one another and, in that one instant, transcended the
struggle it had been to make such an event finally happen.
The conclusion to the ceremony was both ironic and up-
lifting. The assembled guests joined the newlyweds in singing
Jayn's favorite song, "Zip a Dee Doo Dah." As if by some
magic, the words set the tone for the rest of the day: it stayed
sunny, there was much laughter and good feeling, and, thanks
to Tim, an unflappable chef and consummate professional,
the food was nothing short of a culinary coup!

In the process of planning their wedding, the newlyweds
had learned several valuable lessons. Their overly ambitious
plans had far exceeded their combined abilities to see them
through and seriously taxed the limited resources available at

the wedding site. Looking back, Jayn had to admit that theirs was a wedding disaster waiting to happen.

I think that if you are going to do a transplanted wedding, you should do it in terms of what comes with that territory—go native! My wedding was like saying, "Let's go climb Mt. Everest this weekend." It was not a sane thing to do.

But these indomitable newlyweds are convinced of something even greater and more enduring than a one-day celebration. "If you can survive a problem wedding," Jeff declared with certainty, "you can accomplish *anything* together as a couple!" Jayn, nodding her head, lovingly agreed.

Tips from Jayn and Jeff

1. Avoid having to "import" what you need to make your wedding happen. Deal with what is already available at your wedding site—keep things simple.

2. Communicating your creative ideas long distance is difficult to achieve. What may be perfectly clear in your mind, probably isn't in someone else's.

3. Delegate, but still supervise. Even when people make commitments intending to honor them, their follow-through might be different than what you expected.

4. When you *have to have* a certain detail your way or else . . . do it yourself.

5. The minute you leave your "turf" and travel to someone else's, you increase the risk of losing control of your plans.

6. If your wedding didn't happen exactly the way you thought it would, don't get stuck on "what could have been." You can't redo it or relive it—*let it go!*

Whether it is because of an insatiable traveling bug, tender predilections for romance and privacy, family geopolitics, or simply the exhilaration of creating an utterly unique ceremony in an equally unique location, long-distance weddings occupy a category of their own. But have no illusions: if you decide to leave town to tie the knot, expect to encounter special planning issues in addition to those associated with weddings on one's own turf. Few weddings-from-afar are trouble-free. Typically, the error quotient increases with every mile you put between you and your wedding site.

Executing a successful long-distance wedding turns on as many unforeseen factors as foreseen ones. Judy and Abel's large-scale traditional wedding seemed relatively glitch-proof compared with Jayn and Jeff's more ambitiously creative one. What emerges from these two wedding stories are two conclusions. First, that the more creative and the more elaborate your blueprints, the more complicated long-distance planning becomes. And second, the more cosmopolitan your location, the more resources you will have at your fingertips—fax-wise, phone-wise, face-to-face-wise. The opposite is generally true, as your wedding site becomes increasingly more rural and remote.

Also, distance usually means that you'll probably have to rely on other people more than you might if your wedding were taking place where you live. It is also more likely that marrying out of town will force you to delegate more and supervise less. Depending on your personality and planning style, this overall loss of practical and creative control may be irritating and frustrating. Amy and Doug couldn't have been happier with this kind of an arrangement. Could you?

But there are ways to get around these stumbling blocks. The most important thing to remember is that you are not Pharaoh, so try to avoid moving "heaven and earth." Visit the wedding site as often as possible before the wedding so you can anticipate snags and then plan around them. Once you have a realistic idea of what is possible, work with what is on hand and on-site! Be sure to allow a lot of extra time to line up local vendors who will do the job the way you want it done. But don't assume that it will be—designate someone you can trust to follow up! Finally, take a premarital pledge with your bride or groom the night before you are wedding-bound. Promise each other to treasure your long-distance wedding—whether it is "picture-perfect" or not.

CHAPTER 8

~

PMS: Premarital Syndrome

Getting married is one of the biggest changes you'll ever make, a milestone event after which countless aspects of your life will never be the same. Change is almost always accompanied by feelings of uncertainty, so it would be unrealistic to expect to feel otherwise at such a transformative point in your life. It isn't just the stress of planning a wedding that causes brides and grooms to occasionally be at odds; the underlying anxiety about beginning a new life together can also create considerable friction. Even those who've lived together prior to getting married acknowledge the momentous transition that marriage signifies. You are, after all, joining your life to another's. It's no small move.

As you and your future mate undertake the mostly joyous task of creating your wedding, the important thing isn't to avoid conflict but to anticipate it—and learn how to deal with it. Literally hundreds of joint decisions have to be made as you shape this event together, and disagreements are inevitable. Give each other room for moods and emotional swings. Understand that not only is it natural to have different ideas about the ideal wedding, it's also normal for your relationship to be less than ideal right now. Keep lines of communication open, talk things over, try to understand the other person's point of view. And keep your sense of perspective—and sense of humor. After all, the wedding is only the first day of your life together; resolving your differences will be an ongoing process.

When "old married couples" give newlyweds advice, *compromise* is usually the first word mentioned. But as clichéd as it sounds, it's profoundly important. Compromise means that both sides make concessions yet still get part of what they originally wanted. In the course of planning your big day, the wedding you've always fantasized about may clash with the one your fiancé has in mind. So the two of you will be forced to do one of the following:

- come up with a third "vision"
- compromise by combining your two different visions
- let one person "have their way"

Most couples realize that when a particular issue means a lot more to one person than the other, it's probably best to let that person have what they want. If he can't *live* without a salsa band at your reception and you can tolerate one, give him the gift of music. If she's *always* had her heart set on a candlelight ceremony and you'd rather exchange vows out in the woods somewhere, let her have the candles and find some woods when you're on your honeymoon. Part of what makes a wedding ideal is seeing your mate happy and knowing you had something to do with it.

But prewedding difficulties don't always involve disagreements between groom and bride. There are a host of other people whose expectations are riding on your day: parents, relatives, children, friends. What they want for you isn't necessarily what you want for yourself; but if you love them, you'd like them not only to approve of your wedding but to be touched by it in some way as well. Because of its innate significance, a wedding is supposed to be all things to all people. Can you satisfy everyone? Not likely.

But you'll probably try. Even the most relaxed, mature, "together" couple who insists their wedding is about pleasing themselves and the rest of the world be damned, may be alarmed to discover perfectionist tendencies overtaking them as W-Day approaches. Like Maggie in Chapter 3, you could find yourself metamorphosing from a perfectly sensible human being who usually goes-with-the-flow to a possessed creature who stays up all hours of the night worrying that the sparklers in the cake won't ignite, agonizing over how much jumbo shrimp to order, and fretting over whether your best friend, the punk rock singer, will insult your Aunt Ida. Ordinarily none of these things would matter in the least, but this is, after all . . . *your wedding!!!!* And you've only got one shot to get it right.

Or, like Michael in Chapter 3, you may become so overwhelmed by the task of hosting your own wedding that pessimism and negativity don't begin to define your dark mood. The night before the wedding, you torment your fiancée by itemizing everything you *know* will go wrong tomorrow until she wonders what she saw in you in the first place.

At least women with premenstrual syndrome can blame occasional bouts of irrationality, insecurity, and volatility on their hormones. But grooms and brides can point the finger as well. They can blame premarital syndrome on:

- Our culture—which places so much importance on *one single day* that anyone who doesn't go a little crazy has got to be insanely oblivious
- Their parents, friends, and anyone else who doesn't know when *not* to give unsolicited advice
- Their spouse-to-be for not agreeing to elope
- Very real fears about embarking upon a new life

Premarital syndrome can be as minor and fleeting as a one-day "planning overload" migraine or as major and destabilizing as having serious doubts about going through with the marriage. PMS can make you impatient, compulsive, energetic, tense, exhausted, giddy, manic, or depressed.

Like all debilitating syndromes, those afflicted can take

comfort and learn from others who have been there and "recovered." It is in this spirit that we offer the following stories of prewedding anguish—and joy.

Agreeing to Disagree: Diane and Ben

The Bride:	Age 38, first marriage
The Groom:	Age 41, second marriage
Ceremony:	Jewish
Site:	Hotel
Guests:	150
Cost:	$20,000

Diane:

Ben was very involved in every detail. It wasn't like he said to me, "You're the woman, you plan the wedding." He has tastes and opinions about everything, and he wanted to be in charge. Actually, we're both extremely controlling people and we both wanted to be in charge.

Ben:

I have this reputation for being controlling, but in terms of my work life I have to be. I'm a tax lawyer—you can't be lax about tax returns. The interesting thing was that when the chips were down, Diane was the controlling one who wanted every detail orchestrated.

At least Ben and Diane agreed on one thing: they both have a tendency to try to control the other. Theirs is a story of two strong-willed people with different tastes and priorities who had very definite ideas about creating the wedding they wanted. Since neither found it easy to meet the other halfway, they were facing some serious struggles.

Although their wedding planning experience was fraught with conflict, there was also common ground—especially concerning the most significant part of their event, the ceremony. Ben and Diane both knew they wanted a Jewish ceremony that was personalized and inclusive of a feminist point of view. They found a liberal rabbi and a female cantor with whom they met several times to review not only what would be said but what would be sung. The couple emphasized their desire for a ceremony that used nonsexist language and referred to the two of them as individuals.

Assured that the officiants shared their progressive views, Ben and Diane provided them with a number of Hebrew songs to incorporate into the ceremony, and asked the cantor and rabbi to learn them and then submit a "demo tape." This way the bride and groom could make sure they liked how they sounded. To make certain "they weren't singing something like 'Now we're selling this beautiful young bride to her husband for three sheep . . . ,'" Diane asked for translations of the songs she was unfamiliar with.

Diane and Ben were also in complete accord about the wording on their invitations. Because dancing at a Jewish wedding is such a longstanding and joyful tradition, their invitations began: "Diane and Ben invite you to dance at their wedding . . ."

And, finally, the couple saw eye to eye when it came to negotiating the best value for their money and splurging on worthwhile extravagances. "With the hotel, we never accepted anything they said as the way it absolutely had to be," Diane told us. "We're both in business for ourselves, so we know you can negotiate anything." And negotiate they did. Although the hotel usually didn't rent out the main ballroom to groups under three hundred, Diane and Ben convinced them to do so since it was a less busy time of year—between Christmas and New Year's. Thus they got the opulent, high-ceilinged room with crystal chandeliers and huge dance floor for their relatively small gathering of 150 guests.

Diane and Ben agreed on two extravagances: music and flowers. Ben hired an eleven-piece orchestra they had been impressed with at a recent event they'd attended. The top-notch musicians—string section, horns, and a singer—all dressed in tuxes and were an all-around class act. Ben didn't think twice about the two-thousand-dollar fee. In his view, "music that creates a special atmosphere is worth every penny."

Diane also opted for the best—or in this case, the most fragrant—when it came to flowers. She wanted the room to smell wonderful, and therefore chose gardenias and tropical flowers, a delight to both the eye and the nose. The two-thousand-dollar price tag didn't faze her, because scent and beauty were priorities.

Ben got the orchestra he wanted, Diane got the flowers of her choice, and they both negotiated for the most sympathetic officiants and the best room at the hotel. So what caused the problems?

First of all, considerable tension surrounded the decision to get married. Ben had been married before—for nine years. He was twenty-two when that wedding took place, and his parents essentially took charge of all the planning. "I was much younger and wasn't able to pay for a wedding then, so they paid for it and arranged it. Basically it was their show, on their turf."

Doubts about giving up control surfaced once again when he and Diane got engaged some eighteen years later. Thinking it would "get Ben in the mood," a friend lent them a wedding planning video. There were lots of jokes in the video about how the groom typically feels he's losing his freedom, one even compared him to a prisoner on death row! "When the lights came on after the viewing," Diane recalled, "Ben was as white as a sheet, and we didn't talk about getting married for another year."

When that year had passed, the couple was living together and Ben found the idea of planning a wedding—and beginning a second marriage—less intimidating. This time around, he was a mature person who would be paying for the wedding himself—and planning it with his fiancée. "I didn't want my parents involved, because they make me crazy. Diane and I wanted it to be *our* wedding and didn't want them to intrude."

But even without parental interference and with Ben's qualms about remarriage now eased, the couple still had to face their own differences. The first confrontation involved just what kind of wedding they envisioned. It seems Diane's definition of "casual" translated to Ben's notion of "tacky."

Diane:
  *Initially we thought we'd do it kind of low key. I
  had been to a wedding at a nearby recreation center,
  and it was very nice. I wanted our wedding to be a big
  celebration, I wanted to wear a white dress, but I wasn't
  committed to having it at a hotel or a temple. I didn't
  really need a lot of those accoutrements.*

Ben:
  *She wanted to serve macaroni salad and chili. Hippie
  dippie. That might have been great for me in 1967,
  but in the 1990s I didn't want to do that. I always
  maintained that if we were going to have a large wedding,
  we had to have certain minimum standards of classiness.*

Matters of personal aesthetics and taste are subjective and therefore difficult to negotiate. But the more Ben and Diane considered their options, the more Diane understood why Ben felt that a hotel would be more suitable than a rec center: such a special occasion warranted an elegant setting, and a hotel would be more comfortable for the number of guests they had in mind. Diane "came around," with no hurt feelings, no lingering resentments.

The next feud involved the guest list. The battle lines were drawn as follows: Diane wanted to invite "everybody I'd even remotely thought of having at my wedding" and Ben wanted to lay down some ground rules. They created "A," "B," and "C" lists on their computer—A for those people they *had to invite,* such as immediate family; B for those they *really wanted;* and C for those they could *consider excluding.* But it wasn't easy for Diane to shift into the excluding mode.

Diane:
   After we came up with the lists, we had battles, because I was very emotional on this issue. It was my wedding, for God's sake, and Ben had it organized like logarithms! I'm much more impulsive and spontaneous, and I did invite people off the top of my head. I'd come home and tell him, and he'd protest, "Oh, God! You invited another person?"

Ben:
   I kept trying to get her to accept a few rules. One is, if you haven't seen a friend over the last year, then consider not inviting them. The other is, stop and think, would you treat this person to a hundred-dollar meal at a restaurant? And if you wouldn't, why should you treat them to one at your wedding?

Diane halfheartedly cut back on the guest list, but still regrets the compromise. Since the wedding, she has encountered childhood friends and coworkers who were hurt because they weren't invited. In retrospect, Diane claims they should have spent the extra money.
   If you're concerned about finances, resolving a planning dispute on the basis of saving money makes sense—as long as it doesn't shortchange your overall positive feeling about your wedding. Diane confesses that there were really only about seven or eight people she wishes hadn't been cut from the guest list. Otherwise, she concedes that Ben's cost-cutting concerns were warranted.
   When disagreements do not involve money, compromise is

a much bigger problem. A case in point: the selection of taped incidental music to be played prior to Ben and Diane's ceremony. Wanting to create a certain mood, the couple spent days listening to, analyzing, and discussing each musical piece. Attention to detail got way out of hand and heated arguments ensued. Diane recalled the fights:

> We fought over what mood was being established, the significance of certain songs, the political implications of each piece. You get into an altered state of consciousness planning a wedding, where you're fixated on stuff that's very silly and trivial. But when you're in that state of mind you can't let go.

Diane speaks for many of us when she describes how your wedding can turn you into a compulsive fanatic. Believing that every minute item is fraught with meaning, we become obsessed with attempting to make the "proper" decision regarding dozens and dozens of details. Perhaps the most sensible thing to do when you feel yourself agonizing over such choices is to put it aside for a while and gain some perspective. Put off any decision making for an hour—or a week—and try to regain a sense of what your wedding is all about. Most likely it *isn't* about color schemes or carrot cakes or nineteenth-century Russian composers whose music is going to make or break your day.

Still, the notion of just what comprises extreme behavior is subjective. Ben didn't consider unreasonable his suggestion that the two of them sample every prospective menu item for the sit-down dinner. Diane disagreed. And Diane didn't think her proposal to have two rehearsals—one in their actual wedding attire—was excessive. Here's how the two perceived the issue of rehearsing the processional:

Diane:
> Although Ben was insistent that we double-check all sorts of other details, when it came to the ceremony

he didn't think we needed a rehearsal! Since my bridesmaids
were little girls—my nieces—I was going berserk. I wanted
to walk them through it a hundred times. As it turned
out, we didn't get enough time to rehearse and my
brother, who walked me down the aisle, went crazy
right before the processional because he didn't know how
to count out the steps!

Ben:
   Diane wanted the processional to be like a
choreographed stage number. Down to the point where
people would know whether they were putting their left
foot first or their right foot first. And she actually
wanted a preliminary rehearsal and a "dress
rehearsal"—with everybody in their wedding clothes!

An objective third party would probably conclude that Diane and Ben each present convincing arguments. Yes, it's a
good idea to have a wedding rehearsal, especially when
children—and nervous brothers—are involved. And yes, it's
probably going overboard to insist on a "dress rehearsal,"
since participants can learn their parts regardless of what
they're wearing.

Without the aid of a third party, Ben and Diane ended up
compromising. They had the rehearsal but not the dress rehearsal. Perhaps they could have used a little extra time to run
through it, but the processional went off just fine—despite Diane's brother's last-minute panic.

As hard as newlyweds-to-be try to keep themselves on an
even keel, well-meaning (and not so well-meaning) relatives
and friends have a way of contributing to prewedding woes.
In addition to their own skirmishes, Ben and Diane had to
contend with Ben's parents' overzealous desire to be kept
abreast of the latest wedding planning news. Ben was familiar
with and understood his parents' need to be involved. Diane,
on the other hand, perceived her future in-laws' behavior as
intrusive:

*They wanted to get involved with who was going to walk
down the aisle, who was going to stand where, what
the bridesmaids were wearing. Ben would shut down
and not give them a lot of answers and then they would
try to pull it out of me—and give me advice. It was "What
are you serving? Oh, no, you should serve this." Or,
"What time are you starting? No, you should start a
half-hour earlier." Whatever it was, they wanted to have
a say.*

Diane and Ben decided the best way to handle his parents
was to give them something to be in charge of: the rehearsal
dinner. His mom and dad had complete authority over when
and where it would be held, the menu, and other details. Although it didn't prevent them from asking questions, it did
help channel their eagerness to be included.

Meanwhile, Diane's friends were also the source of certain
tensions. Having been part of a close-knit group of single female friends for many years, Diane's upcoming marriage was
seen by some as a betrayal. The circle of friends was almost
like an alternative "family," and now that Diane was about to
break off and create her own, resentful comments were made
about her "selling out" and being spirited away by "some guy."
A few girlfriends also voiced their disapproval by criticizing
the extravagance of Diane's wedding. As if it were any of their
business, they asked, "Wouldn't you rather splurge on a great
honeymoon or save the money for something more important?" Hurt by her friends' disapproval, Diane defended her
decision to have "a big event, a really nice day to remember."

It's unfortunate that those who profess to want the best for
us occasionally make things worse by being critical and judg-
mental. Interjecting their own values and standards, they
seem unable to acknowledge what seems obvious to the rest
of us: that all brides and grooms are entitled to make their
own choices.

One of Ben and Diane's last—and most serious—fights took
place only a week or two before the wedding. During this pe-

riod of time the couple would face each other at the breakfast table each morning with mile-long "To Do" lists and remind the other to take care of this or that detail. Both were nervous about getting everything done in the midst of busy work schedules.

The major confrontation was over a relatively minor issue: where to have the dinner for out-of-town guests, scheduled for the night before the rehearsal dinner. Diane envisioned a casual meal at a local deli. "I wanted the evening to be real loose and easygoing." It would be a chance for the out-of-towners to get together and "talk loud." Ben didn't like the restaurant Diane had in mind. "It was too low class, and symbolized something negative to me—a schmaltzy atmosphere that I didn't want my family from back east to be subjected to." What began as a tense discussion escalated quickly into a full-scale argument. Should the dinner be a quiet evening where people could really get to know each other? A relaxed, boisterous occasion for everyone to enjoy themselves? An opportunity to impress friends and relatives with the couple's host and hostessing skills? It took awhile, but finally tempers cooled, and Diane and Ben reached a compromise: they'd hold the dinner at a deli, but one that was more upscale than Diane's original suggestion.

Looking back on that last premarital altercation, Diane and Ben provided their insights into how such a seemingly insignificant dispute got so out of hand:

Diane:
*During that whole period there was a lot of
tension—making sure everything got done, dealing
with out-of-town relatives and where they were going to
stay. Plus, I guess I had certain doubts about getting married
at this stage in my life. I was thinking, "Oh, my God,
What am I doing? I'm just not the type to get married.
I'm too old, too set in my ways."*

Ben:
*Diane and I have problems resolving conflicts when
we use them as an excuse to generalize about the*

other person's character traits. I can't imagine now why
I was so doctrinaire about not having that dinner at the
deli Diane suggested. It really wasn't such a big deal.

Both Diane and Ben revealed that at the heart of their conflict was a great deal more than the pros and cons of the
neighborhood deli. As with most arguments, there were underlying issues that triggered the escalation of their disagreement. Superficially, Diane was frazzled with last-minute
planning details, but she was also harboring serious doubts
about getting married. Like many older first-time marrieds, Diane was worried that she might be unable to make the transition from a single lifestyle to being permanently part of a
couple. After twentysome years of living on her own, could
she make the adjustment? Granted she and Ben had been living together for a while, but their numerous prewedding quar-
rels weren't helping to lessen her fears.

Ben, in turn, was sensitive about criticism that seemed to hit
below the belt. Disagreeing with the other person's position
was one thing: name-calling and character assault were something else. He was correct in pointing out that resolving differences is impossible when one or both parties use the
argument as an opportunity to insult the other.

Diane and Ben are each very strong personalities, not afraid
to stand up for what they believe in and hold firm with what
they think is right. That's probably part of the reason they were
attracted to one another. It also may account for some of their
disagreements, no matter what the stated cause. But their experience in working through their wedding planning struggles
has taught them a number of lessons: that compromise is possible; that not everything is worth going to battle over; that it's
important to deal with underlying issues; and that a sense of
humor is worth a thousand words.

A booklet entitled *Ben and Diane's Marital Musings*—
containing the seven Jewish marriage blessings, poems, and
an "existential cartoon"—was distributed to guests prior to
Ben and Diane's wedding ceremony. Putting together this

artistic/literary offering was a joint effort, which caused no disputes. One page was entitled "For Ben on Our Wedding Day," and is Diane's original poem, the first stanza of which reads:

We stand under a firmament of flowers
In full bloom.
The space between these poles suggests a home.
Something between us here
Takes a life of its own
Better than either of us.

Tips from Diane and Ben

1. Plan on having more fights than usual. A wedding is an intense experience and emotions can be charged. Keep your sense of humor, agree to disagree, and try to compromise.

2. When you argue, stay focused on the issue and don't allow the dispute to degenerate into generalized character assault.

3. If you're at such odds that you can't imagine either one of you giving an inch, make an agreement to table the issue for at least twenty-four hours. Once you've both cooled down, it will be easier to hear the other person's point of view.

4. When you're dealing with a hotel or any other vendor, don't let the emotionalism of your wedding interfere with your negotiations. Ask questions, pay attention to detail, and approach it like any other business transaction.

5. Ask a friend to help you target gifts that you really want and need. Since we were older and already had a lot of household items, we asked the friend who organized

Diane's shower to have people contribute money toward a "Linens Fund." That was one thing we wanted to start fresh with, and this way we got to choose exactly what we wanted.

6. Don't be afraid to ask the band to play special songs that you'd like to hear—even if they aren't familiar with them. We got some sheet music for an old 1920s Polish Klezmer band tune and had the orchestra members learn it. They were thrilled that we had such a strong interest in music, and we were delighted to have the piece played at our wedding, since it reminded us of our ancestors from Poland.

7. Make sure you know who the maître d' in charge of your room is and get him/her on your side. Tip them generously. It's worth it.

8. Before cutting back on the guest list, make your choices wisely. A few hundred dollars may seem like a big deal now, but it may be worth it not to have regrets later.

First Time Out Versus Second Time Around: Kelly and Howard

The Bride: Age 28, first marriage

The Groom: Age 39, second marriage

Ceremony: Co-officiated Episcopalian and Jewish

Site: Hotel

Guests: 200

Cost: $35,000

Kelly:
I wanted a big wedding both for my family and for me. I wanted to let the world know—my friends, my relatives—that this was the man I was choosing. To celebrate that. To make that commitment socially.

Howard:
It was my second marriage, and I wanted it to be more personal than the first one had been. To be for us as opposed to the families and the generations and the social environment that we were in.

Howard and Kelly's story concerns two issues that many couples must face when planning their wedding: family involvement and expectations associated with first versus second weddings. A great deal of conflict arose over both of these issues because Kelly and Howard felt so differently about them.

Kelly wanted her parents to be part of the planning process and would have been extremely disappointed had she not been able to invite her entire extended family to the wedding. She comes from a large Armenian family with whom she maintains very close ties. Most of her relatives live close by, and family gatherings are a welcome part of her life. Since this was Kelly's first wedding, she had no desire to hold back on any of the traditional embellishments.

Howard was much more anticonventional and skeptical about involving parents in the planning process. He had married for the first time when he was twenty-one and described that wedding as a "big hoopla," with all the standard middle-class trappings. Not only were his and his ex-wife's parents in charge, but nearly every aspect of the wedding was predetermined by custom, leaving him with little—if any—opportunity for input.

It seemed like everything had been decided by the culture, so there was little room left to express any individual anything. There weren't many choices to make at all.

*I guess you could pick a few colors of things, but that's
about it. So this time around, I didn't want to be part
of any of that. I wanted to avoid as many conventions
as possible.*

Howard has since moved away from his hometown. While
he loves his family, he feels his life is separate from theirs. He
questions Kelly's strong connection to her parents and was annoyed that she wanted them to be involved in planning their
wedding. If the choice had been his alone, he would have
opted for an intimate ceremony "in a meadow somewhere"
with just close friends and a few relatives.

But the decision was not his alone. Kelly did not want to
have a small wedding. She was the first among all her cousins
on both sides of her family to get married, so she saw her
wedding as an important event not only for herself and Howard but for her family as a whole.

*Out of the whole second generation of cousins—the children
of all my folks' brothers and sisters—mine was the
first wedding. So the celebration was also for my
parents. It was like their party, too.*

Not only did she want everyone in her huge family to attend, but Kelly had lots of friends and looked forward to "a
big celebratory event with everyone I had grown up with."

And there was another element that figured significantly
into the controversy over Kelly's parents' role: they were paying for most of the wedding. While not all parents who pay for
their daughter's or son's wedding insist on being in charge,
very few relinquish complete control. And because both Kelly
and her family perceived the wedding as being a family event,
her parents weren't about to bow out.

Most of the initial planning sessions involved Kelly, Howard,
and Kelly's mom. Although Kelly claimed she was trying to
play middle woman between her mother and Howard, Howard said he often felt betrayed by Kelly for taking her mother's

position. Here's how differently they each saw the same process:

Howard:
Every step of the way I tried to fight for things that would be more informal and casual and closer to nature. And each time I lost that battle, thinking that Kelly was on my side and then finding out otherwise.

Kelly:
I was caught in the middle and it was really hard and painful. I did a lot of crying because of divided loyalties. I wanted to honor what Howard wanted and I wanted to honor what my mother wanted, and what did I want? I was mixed. On the one hand I thought a meadow might have been nice, but when we discussed it realistically, we would have had to get caterers and rent dozens of tables and chairs, and it would have been very complicated to make it all work. So we compromised.

With a two hundred-person guest list, Kelly concluded that the most sensible site would be a hotel. But wanting to satisfy Howard's desire to have the event outside, she searched for one that had a beautiful outdoor garden area. They settled on one of the loveliest and most secluded hotels in the city, complete with swan-filled lagoons, babbling brooks, and lush flower gardens. The late-afternoon ceremony would take place in the garden, and the sit-down dinner reception would be held in the grand ballroom.

Although Howard was placated by the garden setting, he still felt that many decisions were either railroaded past him by Kelly and her mother, or blatantly made against his wishes. He would have preferred something more casual than a sit-down dinner, for example, but ultimately gave in to majority rule.

On the other hand, Howard and Kelly agreed completely on

several important aspects of the wedding, about which Kelly's parents had no say. One element was the ceremony itself. The couple decided they wanted a co-officiated interfaith ceremony that would incorporate both the Christian and Jewish religions. Although it would have been easier to arrange a ceremony using either one officiant or the other, neither Kelly nor Howard wanted that. Howard explained why:

> We liked the idea of honoring both faiths. I wanted to identify with my Jewish background, and it felt stronger to also respect Kelly's religion, as opposed to trying to make one or the other of us "cave in." We preferred having the strengths of each.

Unfortunately, the Armenian church with which Kelly's family is affiliated doesn't allow interfaith marriages, nor does the Conservative branch of the Jewish religion, in which Howard was brought up. In fact, Kelly and Howard had difficulty finding even a reform rabbi and a liberal priest who would consent to co-officiate. After time-consuming research and numerous phone calls, they finally located a rabbi and an Episcopalian priest who were good friends and function as a team at interfaith ceremonies. The couple met briefly with the officiants and, relieved that they agreed to perform the ceremony, left the content up to them.

Music was the other joint decision that the couple made in complete accord. Howard is a die-hard rhythm and blues fan, and Kelly wanted music that celebrated her cultural roots. So they hired both an "r & b" band *and* a group of authentic Armenian musicians, and decided to switch back and forth throughout the evening. Their guests would be treated to an exhilarating night of intercultural dancing!

Meanwhile, there was still conflict surrounding a host of other details. At the root of it all was Howard's resistance to anything that smacked of traditional wedding etiquette, because he'd had enough conventionality at his first wedding; and Kelly's frustration at having to battle with him over every minor issue. Fights would erupt over a particular concern and, rather than work out a compromise that was agreeable to both of them, one person would grudgingly "give in." Kelly described their clash over whether or not to have a receiving line:

> *I remember crying, wishing Howard wasn't so difficult. He went on and on about not wanting a receiving line, that it was too artificial, too formal. So we didn't have one, and what happened as a result was that I never got to see everybody who came to the wedding. I felt bad, because it was important to me to make a connection to people, and I couldn't get to everybody during the course of the wedding.*

Howard defended his position this way:

> *I just think that a receiving line is another symbol of people joining in a formal manner. And I don't think that's what a wedding is really about. I think it's spiritual and romantic and, in the end, that's what matters. The other is not important, so why give it any legitimacy?*

Again, an unbiased third party would conclude that both positions have some validity. Although formality shouldn't take precedence over the spiritual or romantic aspects of a wedding, it often serves a very practical purpose.

The question of photography also brought up the issue of formality versus informality, as well as Howard's negative experiences from his first wedding. And once again, he and Kelly's mother were at loggerheads. She wanted to chronicle the event with traditional group photographs of family members. Howard wanted only candid photos.

> *I remember from my first wedding that those formal shots were the only pictures we had. They took a long time and spoiled the mood. And it meant taking time away*

*from informally greeting people. So more time was spent
doing more formal things.*

This time the opposing sides were able to work out a solution acceptable to both: a few posed, group shots would be taken immediately following the ceremony, but the photographer would do his best to work quickly so that everyone could proceed to the reception. Candid shots would also be taken throughout the evening.

Very few brides and grooms see eye to eye on every aspect of planning their wedding; at some point differences of opinion, taste, and outlook surface to create a struggle. But Kelly and Howard disagreed fundamentally on several crucial matters which made equitable resolution difficult. Howard's first wedding turned him off of convention entirely. What he envisioned this time around was a very casual, intimate celebration. But as a first-time bride, Kelly wanted to retain certain traditions. Although she wasn't interested in having bridesmaids, a best man, or maid of honor ("I felt we were the ones getting married and that we should stand alone at the altar"), her fantasy did include a lavish party surrounded by all her family and friends. She and Howard both tried to appease the other, but their gut feelings about the kind of wedding they wanted were so dissimilar that one or the other often ended up feeling slighted.

So what ultimately came out of their attempts to work through these differences? And what did they learn about each other and themselves as a couple?

Kelly:
   *It was a real awakening in terms of who I had
chosen as a mate. What I love about Howard is that
he's strong-willed and has these beliefs. That's why I married
him—he's interesting and feisty and an independent thinker.
But he's really difficult to be with and live with at
times, too. So it's a double-edged thing. Also, my
loyalty to my family has been an ongoing battle.*

*But the wedding taught me that Howard and I will
survive—that we can be so at odds and so angry and
yet still have plenty of good stuff that keeps us going.*

Howard:
*When you're dating someone or even living with them,
you're under the illusion that it's just them that you're
with. But Kelly has such a strong family, I think I
should have realized that they have a lot of power.
And part of Kelly is getting along with everybody; she
would never want to alienate them.*

*Still, even when we were having all those fights,
I never felt that it was about the real important things
between Kelly and me. All the customs that our culture
spends so much time on aren't what's really important.
What counts in the end is the spiritual connection
between the two of you.*

The day of Kelly and Howard's wedding, guests gathered in
the hotel garden before the ceremony and listened to the me-
lodious mandolin-like strains of an Armenian "oud." The ceremony commenced with the rabbi's portion of the service, after
which the priest took over. According to Howard and Kelly, he
got a bit off-track, launching into "this bizarre political speech
about pollution and you name it. It had nothing to do with
us." As the "crazy sermon" seemed to go on ad infinitum,
Howard and Kelly exchanged panicked looks. Howard was
about to say something when a hummingbird appeared—as a
kind of sign. "I thought, 'Well, at least God's here in some way
anyway,' and I just let the priest finish." It turns out the priest
had imbibed a little too much wine prior to the ceremony, but
Howard and Kelly didn't let his "very unique" service keep
them from enjoying their party.

Following the ceremony, the immediate families had "just a
few" group photos taken and then headed indoors to join
their guests for cocktails and sushi hors d'oeuvres. After an elegant sit-down dinner, the festivities got seriously underway. In

between rock-out rhythm and blues, traditional Armenian tunes blared as men and women formed separate circles for folk dancing—with Kelly in the center of the women's circle and Howard at the core of the men's. The bands played on into the night.

In the end, Kelly and Howard's wedding more closely resembled Kelly's fantasy than Howard's. The fact that her family had such a great stake in hosting a huge celebration tipped the scales in her favor. But certainly concessions were made to assure that Howard would be happy as well: the garden, the r & b band, fewer formalities. Interestingly, Kelly conceded that, if it were her second marriage instead of her first, the wedding would have been very different:

I think a lot of the conflicts were because it was my first marriage and Howard's second. If I were to get married again, it would be . . . in a meadow! Smaller, more intimate, just close friends. Actually, very similar to what Howard was fighting for!

Tips from Kelly and Howard

1. Remember that your wedding is not as important as your relationship. Regardless of the fights that arise in the course of planning your wedding, what ultimately matters is the connection between the two of you.

2. Working through conflicts is a good way to learn about each other and what you're going to have to deal with in the context of your marriage.

3. If it's clear at the outset that your ideas about the ideal wedding are so different it will be impossible to compromise, it's better to decide up front which person's concept you'll go with—or come up with a third one

that appeals to both of you. This will prevent numerous battles along the way.

4. Try to separate what happened at your first wedding from what will happen at this one. After all, different people are involved . . . and this is a different time in your own life as well.

Every Conflict Tells a Story

"PMS" can manifest itself in a multitude of ways and strikes newlyweds-to-be regardless of gender, age, or previous marital status. The distress that knocks grooms and brides off-center may be serious or slight, and proven "remedies" range from simple daily exercise to premarital counseling. The following collected tales of prenuptial emotional turmoil were told to us by the various couples we interviewed for this book.

Polar Opposites

What had Ken and Eileen very much on edge prior to their wedding was the question of being on time. And they couldn't be farther apart on this issue. Ken is "extraordinarily time conscious" and was apprehensive about the wedding starting promptly—with good reason. Eileen admits to being consistently late and refused to be pressured about her lack of punctuality. "If we allow enough time, I'm hoping everything will just flow, but I don't want Eileen to be panting as she's coming down the aisle," Ken told us.

Our interview took place before their wedding, so we don't know how prompt Eileen was or how anxious Ken felt prior to the ceremony. But it sounded as if both were edging toward compromise. Eileen said she would try to hold up her side of the bargain by being reasonably on time, and Ken was attempting to be flexible by allowing that 15 minutes was "acceptably late."

Old Fears, Old Memories

The experience of writing their wedding vows together triggered unexpected fears in Samantha about being swallowed up as she had been in her first marriage. When Craig was critical of what she'd written, Samantha interpreted that to mean "Now I'm going to have to fight for everything that is me!" Although they had had years of experience settling their differences, this particular joint decision was especially crucial, because they wanted the vows to be an expression of what was most meaningful about their relationship.

As it happened, Samantha and Craig had started therapy about two months before the wedding as a "preventative measure," and when the issue of the vows arose, their therapy sessions heated up. Whatever rough edges existed between them came to the forefront, but as Craig reported, "We tolerated the anxiety and pain and worked out what was stirring in us."

Insecurities and Doubts

Charlotte was overcome by a host of irrational fears on the morning of her wedding: she was too old to be getting married again; this marriage, like her previous ones, wouldn't work out; David would change his mind. "As much as I wanted to be easygoing, all these thoughts occurred to me within a millisecond." She let herself feel the emotion of it all, cried, and, after she got dressed, felt much better. While she was upstairs with her last-minute doubts, David was downstairs waiting for the guests to arrive. His reflections are testimony to just how little Charlotte actually had to worry about:

*I sat out on the patio of the hotel and quietly realized
what was about to happen. Not one moment of panic
or trepidation or fear came up; I was never so sure
of anything in my life. I think the true test of loving someone
is how they make you feel about yourself, and Charlotte
has made me feel something good that I've never felt
before. I'm no fool—I'm not going to run away from
that!*

Stage Fright

Nancy was surprised by her relatively calm state of mind in
the weeks and days leading up to her wedding. Even with the
whole family getting in the act of planning the event, she said
she trusted that whatever happened, it would be beautiful.

*Unlike my first wedding when my ex-husband and I were
in charge of everything, I was so relieved to have lots
of help this time around that I made a conscious
decision to accept however it turned out. And not to sound
corny, but I was so happy to be marrying Matt that the
wedding itself was secondary.*

Matt was surprised by his emotional state, too. But for the
opposite reason. Usually very relaxed in social situations, he
found himself getting nervous the week before the wedding.
Matt likened the feeling to stage fright:

*I had been taking everything in stride for weeks and then
all of a sudden it dawned on me that Nancy and I
were going to be the focus of all this attention. We
were going to be center stage for an entire day! It's funny,
because I don't consider myself a shy person at all, but
the thought of going public with something that
seemed so personal to Nancy and me suddenly made
me very anxious.*

Matt came up with a simple way to combat those last-minute anxiety attacks; he ran them off. Previously, he had been a sporadic runner, but he intensified his regimen and ran at least two miles every morning before breakfast. "The early-morning exercise was a great way to calm my nerves . . . and the wedding gave me the kick I needed to stick to my routine!"

Major Panic Attack

The normal worry about everything going smoothly was on Don's mind as he waited for Anne to come down the aisle. But if he had known what was going on behind the scenes as he stood there, his anxiety level would have risen dramatically. Anne was having a very uncharacteristic "major panic attack."

The music was playing, Don was standing there, the guests were all waiting . . . and I'm in this little bedroom with my maid of honor going "Oh God, am I really doing this?" We finally made it out the door, and I started to get so nervous that I made myself do "crosscrawl" exercises—where you lift your arms and legs very high and in opposition, to keep your right and left brain intact. So there I was, all dressed up in my dress and heels and everything, doing these crosscrawls and trying to calm myself down. I knew I must have looked ridiculous, but it was the only thing I could think of to alleviate my anxiety.

Overanxious Child of the Bride

Compared to Heidi's four-year-old son, Nathan, bride and groom Heidi and Bruce were downright tranquil. It seems Nathan had a preschool version of "PMS." He was so excited about the upcoming wedding that his level of "hyperness" surpassed both Christmas and birthday party proportions. Similar to Matt's PMS remedy, the proper dose of physical exercise was required to offset Nathan's excess nervous energy. Heidi explained how they handled it:

> *Nathan was literally bouncing off the walls the week before the wedding! We did our best to stick to his regular routines, read him calming bedtime stories, and get him to bed on time. And most important, we made sure that he spent plenty of time outside riding his bike and running around so that he could work off some of that boundless energy!*

Last-Minute "Detailmania"

Leslie characterized Mark as Mr. Calm and herself as Ms. Tense just prior to the wedding. But that was because she was dealing with most of the planning details herself—going over last-minute changes with the caterer and florist and negotiating with the photographer. Leslie also admits that she's much more detail-oriented than Mark, who tends to trust that things will somehow work out. "I would think of something I'd forgotten and say to Mark, 'Oh, my God, what about . . .' and he'd just answer, 'It'll be fine.' "

Having a "pre-honeymoon" two days prior to their wedding—in a secluded cottage suite near where the event was held—helped considerably. The night before the wedding, the couple walked back to their hillside retreat after dinner, had massages, and were soothed by the peaceful, isolated surroundings.

There's no denying the fact that weddings are exciting. And often the line between prewedding excitement and prewedding anxiety is very shady. Looking forward to the first day of your married lives together, it's natural for you and your fiancé to be thrilled—and worried.

Weddings are also a lot of work, and fertile ground for tension and conflict. If you make it through the planning stages of yours without premarital stress of any kind, consider yourselves fortunate. But also keep in mind that part of what creates wedding anxiety is something very positive: the life change you're about to make. Respect that, celebrate it . . . and savor the excitement!

Tips for Coping with Premarital Syndrome

1. Understand that, regardless of your normal state of mind, you will both get a little crazy during this period. Rather than being critical of each other's "altered states," be tolerant—and make a concerted effort to relax.

2. Accept the fact that you and your fiancé will have disagreements in the course of planning your wedding. Just because your visions of the perfect wedding don't match doesn't mean you're ill-suited or love each other any less.

3. Compromise if you can. If you can't, let the person to whom a particular issue means the most have it their way.

4. Since a lot of premarital tension is caused by being overwhelmed with "wedding work," try to divide it as equally as possible between the two of you. Otherwise, resentment builds and conflict is inevitable.

5. Get as much outside help with the "wedding work" as you can. Choose competent people, check in with them as you need to, and then *stop worrying* and trust that those you've chosen will come through.

6. Treat yourself like an athlete in training. Eat healthy, and get plenty of rest and exercise. It will do wonders to lower your stress quotient.

7. Keep your sense of perspective. As meaningful as your wedding day is, it's not as important as the relationship between the two of you. Don't lose sight of what this event is all about.

8. If the tension between you becomes unmanageable, consider seeing a counselor or psychologist. An objective third party trained to work with couples can help you work through conflicts and prevent problems from escalating.

9. Don't lose your sense of humor. Calamity strikes millions of brides and grooms, and they survive. What if you trip going down the aisle? Your wedding cake caves in? The officiant had one too many drinks before the ceremony? Laugh it off. It's only your wedding day . . .

CHAPTER 9

Post-Wedding Letdown and the Honeymoon Cure

The party's over. The guests have all gone home. You did it. You're married. Now what? After the seemingly endless weeks, months (sometimes years!) of masterminding, anticipating, and knocking yourselves out, it's all over in a day, leaving some newlyweds feeling a bit, well . . . let down. It's normal to feel slightly deflated after such a landmark occasion. After all, how can you top a once-in-a-lifetime, blow-out celebration over which you and your new spouse reign as queen-and-king-for-a-day? Once you've played a starring role in humankind's most meaningful festivity, what's left?

The honeymoon.

honey *n.* sweetness, pleasantness, a sweet thing.
moon *v.* to move or look or pass time dreamily or listlessly. [*Oxford American Dictionary*, New York: Avon, 1980, pp. 420, 577.]

Before the sexual revolution of the late 1960s and early 1970s, the honeymoon was usually the first time newlyweds made love to each other. Coy references to lustful couples sequestered in honeymoon suites for days on end without a breather were common. Mothers-of-the-bride took their virginal daughters aside and shyly offered what advice they could. Girlfriends-of-the-bride showered the wife-to-be with an alluring negligee for her first connubial night . . .

How times have changed. In the 1990s, about fifty percent of women ages twenty-five to thirty-four have lived together with a man before they marry; seventy-five percent of women have sex by age nineteen; and the average man loses his virginity at age seventeen.

Does this mean that, for today's newlyweds, sex is nothing to get worked up over? Are sexy honeymoons out? Not at all. Even if couples have been living together before the ceremony or have had previous honeymoons, most still fantasize about this special time alone. Some report feeling a "high" right after their wedding; elated by their new status as husband and wife, they're primed for a uniquely passionate experience. Unlike newlyweds of bygone eras, it's most likely not the "first time" for either one of them, but it *is* the "first-time-as-husband-and-wife." And "firsts" are always thrilling.

But there's more to honeymoons than sex. This initial getaway together is a one-time-only interlude between your wedding and married life. You may take wonderfully romantic second honeymoons in the years to come, but none will take the place of this particular transition in your relationship. Most couples discover that a honeymoon is at least one or more of the following:

- A time to relax after the pressures of planning a wedding
- A time to celebrate the beginning of your marriage . . . alone!
- A time to adjust to the idea of marriage without the intrusion of day-to-day life
- The perfect excuse to take a great vacation!

Honeymooning is also the ideal therapy for post-wedding letdown. Yes, weddings are a hard act to follow, but now is your chance to focus on the two of you for a change, rather than the myriad details that hounded you up until that last handful of rice. On your honeymoon you don't have to worry about alienating your new in-laws, looking picture-perfect for the ubiquitous videographer, or having cake stuffed in your mouth whether you like it or not. It's a time for pleasing only each other.

And for those rare grooms and brides who don't *need* a cure, who felt neither uptight nor let down throughout the entire wedding process: your honeymoon will be the icing on the cake.

Real Honeymoons

Young girls dream about it, little boys joke and giggle over it. We all grow up with the message that our honeymoon will be one of the most breathtakingly perfect times in our life. Hidden away with the one we love in an utterly exquisite setting, we'll blissfully wile away the hours in our temporary nirvana until "the honeymoon's over."

But what are *real* honeymoons like? What are the essentials of a "perfect" one? Can you have one without leaving town . . . or your own home? What's more important: location or state of mind?

In this chapter our creative couples will divulge the real-life answers to these and other questions:

- Are remarrieds just as likely to indulge in a romantic honeymoon? Or do they have a tendency to neglect romance the second time around?
- Can professional couples with busy schedules afford *not* to take a honeymoon?
- What if your ideas about the "ideal honeymoon" are so opposite from those of your mate that you're considering taking separate ones?

- How do you prepare your children for a vacation they *won't* be taking with you?
- Is there room in a petite budget for a memorable honeymoon?

Our couples ran the gamut of honeymoon experiences, choices, and styles—from yoga retreats to package tours, from country-hopping in Europe to holing up in a local motel. Some took their honeymoon before the wedding; others had to delay theirs until many months after the ceremony. A number of couples could afford only a mini-honeymoon close to home; a few jumped on a jet and traveled halfway around the world. There were sun-lovers who took the typical tropical island honeymoon, privacy fiends who insisted on the most secluded cottage in the grove, and exotica devotees who vacationed in unusual locales. And one couple is still waiting for their ship to come in so they can take off on the honeymoon of their dreams . . .

The Mini-Honeymoon

Sure, you'd love to escape to Bali for two weeks, where your most pressing decision would be whether to snorkle in the crystalline blue waters or have another tropical drink delivered to your well-appointed thatched hut. But back in the real world, it'll be months before you're through paying for the wedding, and the work deadlines you promised to forget during the ceremony continue to haunt you. You are not alone. Many newlyweds have neither the time nor the money to take lengthy vacations. But that doesn't mean you can't have a honeymoon. Although short jaunts may not fit the travel-agency definition of "honeymoon getaway," they can still include the essentials of a relaxing, romantic holiday: time away from your established routine and the chance to be alone together.
Anne and Don, the "1950s sock-hop" couple, were limited

by both work schedules and finances. Although Don fantasized about flying off with his new bride to an exotic island halfway around the globe, they could only afford a weekend honeymoon in Santa Barbara, a beautiful seaside town 100 miles up the coast from their home in Los Angeles. Anne's girlfriend gave them their first night in the motel as a wedding gift and had a bottle of champagne waiting for them when they arrived. Even though the couple had visited Santa Barbara on a number of previous occasions, their honeymoon stay was definitely special.

Exhausted but exhilarated after hosting their own wedding, they spent the evening reliving the events of the day. "We giggled about the wedding the whole time, talked about the people who had been there, chuckled about different things that had happened," Don recalled. Relieved to have the wedding work over with, he described their brief but romantic vacation as "a decompression period and a time of intimacy." After weeks of hectic activity, they were obligation-free and alone at last—even if it was only a weekend. And Anne valued that. "It was like . . . God, it's all over! Now, let's just enjoy this little time and space together." A forty-eight-year-old second-time bride, Anne is testimony to the fact that remarriers can be every bit as romantically inclined as those who've never married or honeymooned before.

Don and Anne wished they could have taken longer and gone somewhere farther away, "so that it would have felt like a real escape." But the trip's short duration and familiar surroundings didn't dampen their spirits. In fact, they brought their honeymoon excitement home with them. "It was fun to come back home with the realization that 'Now we're married!' " said Anne. "We hadn't opened our wedding gifts yet, so doing that together kept us in the wedding spirit."

Chapter 2's Nancy and Matt ("A Collective Effort") confess that their "twenty-four-hour honeymoon" was the result of improper planning. When they were deciding which June weekend would be the best for their wedding, a number of considerations were factored in. But leaving enough time for a honeymoon somehow got lost in the shuffle. "We were so focused on figuring out which friends and relatives would be able to make it on which dates and making sure we had enough time to plan the wedding, that we forgot to think about our honeymoon," Nancy admitted. Thus, she had to begin teaching summer school the Monday following their Saturday wedding. It would have been difficult for her to get out of the teaching stint once she'd signed on to do it, and besides, the newlyweds needed the extra money.

Although they had only a day to get away, at least Matt and Nancy knew how to do it up right. They reserved the honeymoon suite at one of Boston's most elegant old hotels, forty-five minutes from Matt's parents' home where the wedding took place. Because they were only staying one night, they could afford to splurge not only on the finest room but on whatever their hearts desired in the way of food and drink. "We had so little time that we decided not to leave the luxury or privacy of our suite, even for our meals," Matt said. "Instead, we made slaves of room service. We never got dressed . . . just waited under the sheets until the silver carts arrived. It was a short honeymoon, but ideal in its own way."

Nancy agreed that their honeymoon was wonderful, what there was of it. But she regretted that it was over so quickly. Having so little time between the wedding and her job made it seem like the honeymoon never happened. "If I had it to do over," she told us, "I would allow at least three or four days for a honeymoon. We had a beautiful night together but had to pack up and leave the following afternoon! You're in a world of your own right after the wedding, and I just wish we could have held on to that a little longer before going back to the real world."

When Leslie and Mark, the interfaith couple from Chapter 4, planned their wedding they knew they wouldn't be able to go on a honeymoon afterward because Mark was scheduled to begin rehearsals for a play, and Leslie would still be in the midst of finishing graduate school. To tide them over until they took their delayed honeymoon in Hawaii, they had a three-day mini-honeymoon before, during, and immediately after their wedding festivities. Theirs, you'll recall, was the day-long wedding at a rented estate, complete with pool party and picnic; volleyball and lawn croquet; ceremony, dinner, and dancing.

For three days their honeymoon hideout was at an exclusive resort near the wedding site. Leslie had heard about the place from friends and, six months prior to their wedding, arranged to drive up the coast with Mark to check it out. They fell in love with the charming cottages nestled in the lush, pastoral hillside and then and there booked the one farthest up the hill and most remote from "civilization." Like Nancy and Matt, because Leslie and Mark had so little honeymoon time, they wanted to make the most of it.

Leslie and Mark's not-by-the-book idea for their "before, during, and after" honeymoon established a closeness between them and also made the entire experience feel more organic. They created a honeymoon for themselves in the midst of their wedding and turned their three days together into an intimate celebration. "It wasn't segmented or linear as in 'Now we do this, now it's time for that,' " Leslie stated. "Instead, it was the sense that the wedding and our honeymoon could all happen at once. We were there by ourselves in this beautiful setting, then joined our friends, swam, and got married and had this fabulous dinner, danced all night, and afterward went back to our little cottage where we still had two more nights together. So it was a very concentrated period of time. No rice, no shoes, no driving away with people shouting."

Mark considered the whole weekend of getting married "a honeymoon, with the wedding in the middle." And he contended that, contrary to established custom, being together the night before the wedding was a plus. "I don't go for this 'Don't look at the bride before the wedding' business, because it's very important to have time alone together *before* the wedding. When we arrived at the wedding we were emotionally prepared for it. We had stayed together in that cottage. We had not been kept separate. We were already a couple."

When it came time to leave the quiet isolation of their honeymoon bungalow, Leslie found herself dreading reentry into normal life. After three intimate days with Mark, she felt "so coupled-up with him." Now he would be out of town working on his play and she would be back in graduate school, alone. The drawbacks of a mini-honeymoon were becoming apparent. As close as they had grown during their short stay at the hillside resort, the time had gone by too quickly. It was all over too soon. "That last morning I was in a funky mood," Leslie confessed. "I felt like I was being torn away from Mark. And I was mad. As we were driving home, he said, 'I wonder how rehearsal is going . . .' and I just thought, 'That's it, it's over. His mind is somewhere else. The honeymoon's officially over.' "

The disadvantage of mini-honeymoons is obvious: they're not long enough. Just when you're beginning to unwind and feel connected to each other, it's time to leave. And returning to normal routines can be more difficult because, like Leslie, you may feel "torn away" from an unfinished experience. Still, mini-honeymoons are better than no honeymoon at all. Like longer ones, they create memories you can indulge in throughout your life . . . for as long as you like.

The At-Home Honeymoon

A stay-at-home honeymoon? Isn't that a contradiction in terms? The whole objective is to take a romantic break from the status quo, get out of town, at least get out of the house— right??? Yes, no, and not necessarily. Certainly staying home isn't most people's idea of the ideal honeymoon; but when circumstances don't permit you to leave town and you can't afford the weekend rates at a local hotel, it's possible to enjoy a post-wedding vacation in the privacy of your own home. You'll need:

- Uninterrupted time together
- An unplugged phone
- Imagination

The point is to carve out a period of time following the wedding during which everything you do is pleasurable, out-of-the-ordinary, and just for the two of you. Take a candlelight bath in jasmine-scented bath oil. Put on a favorite CD and give each other massages. Outfit your bed in some of those new satin sheets you registered for and stay in it for a few days. Slip into the sexy his and hers underwear you've been saving for just this occasion. Order in an exotic cuisine you don't usually eat. Dance.

No one says you can't leave the house during your at-home honeymoon, just don't do errands or go anywhere you usually do. Pretend your city or town is a place you've never visited before. Head for a part of town you don't ordinarily frequent and buy each other souvenirs. Get dressed up and go out to breakfast, lunch, or dinner in a restaurant you've never heard of. Act like a tourist and have drinks at a posh hotel bar or discover an obscure museum you never knew existed. Treat yourselves to tickets to a play, concert, or comedy club. Drive to the beach, lake, woods, or city park and make out. Rent bikes or roller skates or a canoe. Leave home at midnight and explore your city by night. Have coffee and donuts at a truck stop on the outskirts of town. Be adventurous. Indulge yourselves. Have fun.

Honeymooning is a state of mind.

To prove it, let your imagination do the traveling. Kick back on your front steps with a morning cappuccino or afternoon ice-cold margarita and plan the incredible honeymoon you'll take when you get a raise, win the lottery, or hit the big time. Have travel agencies, state travel bureaus, and/or foreign consulates send you tantalizing brochures that you and your honey can moon over while making future plans. Talk about what you would most want to do and see and eat on this mother-of-all-vacations, remembering that this is an exercise in *fantasy*. Even if you may never be able to afford such a dream trip, you can still roll it over in your minds. Imagining a fun time is almost as much fun as having it, especially when you can share the daydream with the one you love. And in conjunction with an at-home honeymoon, it's the next-best thing to being there.

Alicia and Michael are a good case in point. Unable to take a honeymoon trip due to lack of funds and work deadlines, they enjoyed the simple pleasures of being together after the wedding. Once all their guests had left, they stayed up into the wee hours toasting each other and opening presents in the bedroom. The next day was back to work for both of them. Yet the two were so thrilled they both walked around the house shouting, "We're married! We're married!" And they had a great time envisioning the fantasy honeymoon they're going to take as soon as one of them gets lucky—better make that honeymoon*s*. Alicia wants to go to Monte Carlo " 'cause I can gamble and speak French and live on the beach." And Michael's ideal spot would be the Scottish Highlands, "out in the mountains where there's nobody else around . . . or possibly England and from there maybe Italy . . ."

Even if you don't travel any farther than your own living room, you can still catch the honeymoon spirit. All you have to do is give up your day-to-day mindset, grab your honey, and spiritually cruise off somewhere you both long to go. In celebration of the beginning of your life together, give each other the ultimate wedding gift: the feeling that anything's possible.

Vegging Out Versus Venturing Forth

When it comes to conceiving of the perfect honeymoon, one newlywed's dream is another's nightmare. The thought of sightseeing can be hell when all you want to do is plop into a lounge chair and contemplate the deep blue sky; and lying on the same beach day after day is enough to drive adventurous types bonkers. If you're a tennis nut and your spouse wants you to give up your game for three weeks so you can honeymoon in Paris, you might consider that cruel and unusual punishment; and coaxing a confirmed nonathlete to sign up for a white-water rafting expedition would be equally insensitive. So forget the notion of the generic "ideal honeymoon"; it's in the eye of the betrothed.

Vegging Out

For Eileen and Ken—alias "The Groom Who Loved Details"—mellowing out "in paradise" is the number one priority. Once they get to Maui, they want complete privacy and zero plans.

"We've worked so hard to afford this wedding," Eileen told us. "Ken's twelve-hour days and my ten-hour ones entitle us to some serious relaxation!" The newlyweds are not going to stress themselves out with an agenda. What they've got planned is ... nothing at all! "Ken is usually so 'schedule, schedule, schedule,'" Eileen explained, "that on our honeymoon we must wanna do what we wanna do. And as soon as we get to Hawaii, we're talking 'no forwarding address!'" Ken seconded that emotion: "We're just going to rest. No tours, no island-hopping. We'll be married and in paradise ... what more could we want?"

Cynthia and Carl, Chapter 2's "Produced and Directed by Us" team had similar objectives when it came to planning their honeymoon: seclusion and a peaceful setting. After spending their first night in an elegant bed and breakfast in San Francisco (just across the Golden Gate Bridge from their mountaintop wedding site), they brunched with out-of-town family and then headed 125 miles south to Big Sur where Cynthia's parents own a cliffside vacation home overlooking the Pacific.

A dramatically exquisite environment with very little commercial development, Big Sur was the perfect retreat. Cynthia and Carl were completely alone amid the crashing waves and sheltering cypress. And they didn't have to travel far to get there or spend anything to stay there. "I travel so much for work," Cynthia explained, "that I didn't want to go anywhere far away. The place in Big Sur was like having an estate of our own right on the ocean: simple and rustic, but beautiful. We wanted to just be quiet and not see anybody." One night the couple went out to dinner, but otherwise they spent the week hiking in the woods, enjoying nature, and just being together.

"I think the location is critical," Carl added. "It has to be a place that serves a certain purpose. For us it was a time to 'come down' from the production of the wedding and concentrate on being connected."

Returning to nature also had a calming effect on Chapter 3's "Bed and Breakfast Vows" couple, Maggie and Gerry, who spent their honeymoon in Maine. When they first got there, Maggie was so stressed out from the wedding she told Gerry she needed "both a chiropractor and a psychiatrist!" But after several days of pampering themselves in the quiet splendor of first-rate hotels, things began to look up. They just needed to put the wedding frenzy behind them and reconnect. "We fell in love really hard when we first met," Maggie recalled, "and we got married because we can't live without each other. On the honeymoon just being together—and free from all the planning—was wonderful." Gerry agreed that their honeymoon requirements were very simple. Before deciding on Maine, he had "horrible visions" of honeymoon packages, heart-shaped beds, and structured fun. "We didn't want or need all that," he added honestly, "just each other."

Those who opt for the laid-back honeymoon realize that "the basics"—a beautiful setting, privacy, and each other—can be supremely pleasurable. Forget frenetic activity, superfluous sightseeing, and extravagant excursions. Rest revitalizes. Simple is sublime. Less is more.

Venturing Forth

Seclusion, tranquillity, and lazing around aren't appealing to some couples. Even if they are exhausted from their wedding, wanderlust is their passion. On their first official vacation as husband and wife, these newlyweds want nothing more than to hit the open road, set out for parts unknown, or follow the call of the wild. Discovery, adventure, physical activity, or the pursuit of special interests are the essence of their post-wedding plans. Whatever the conveyance—car touring, trekking by foot, rafting, riding the rails, camel caravans—the journey is an end in itself.

Padmini and Michael, the Sri Lankan-English-Irish-Polish-American couple in Chapter 4, seamlessly combined their love for wide open spaces and urbane tastes on their two-and-a-half week honeymoon. Masterminded from beginning to end by Michael, the entire trip was a surprise to his new bride. "The honeymoon was my thing," Michael said proudly, "I wanted it to flow from one location to another with a full range of highs and lows." Just so Padmini would know what to pack, he casually dropped a clue or two a few days before the wedding.

All Padmini was certain about was that she would be spending her wedding night in a local hotel surrounded by "sheer and total indulgence." From then on, each day was like a mysterious gift unfolding. The next morning the newlyweds boarded the plane for the American Southwest. Close enough to fit their budget, but worlds away from their day-to-day life in the big city. "New Mexico has a wonderful romantic mix of the serene, the mystical, and the rustic," Padmini remarked with a beaming smile. "It's big and you are little!"

Their car tour began in Albuquerque where the honeymooners stayed in a quaint hotel that reeked of the Old

West—brass beds, creaky wood floorboards, and "early sa-
loon" decor. Then the two drove to Santa Fe where they spent
the next two days strolling through art galleries, shopping for
Native American jewelry, and sampling the stellar regional cuisine available in the town's trendy restaurants. The next week
was devoted to rest and recovery at a desert guest ranch overlooking a vast mesa. Padmini and Michael set an unrushed
pace horseback riding, hiking, swimming, and sunset watching! Next, the newlyweds drove the winding road north to
Taos through the Sangre de Cristo mountains. There they
switched gears again, visiting the timeless Taos Indian Pueblo,
ancient ruins, and making a day pilgrimage to the home of
D. H. Lawrence.

This kaleidoscope of experiences, shifting moods, and dramatic landscapes are etched into Padmini and Michael's honeymoon memories. The trip oozed romance. So does their
marriage. According to Padmini, "We had a wonderful love affair before we got married and the honeymoon just wrapped
that feeling up and carried it through into our lives."

Honeymoons are a bridge into a new phase of life together,
bringing forward the best of what we have to offer to our
spouse. Although we don't plan our marriages the way we
plan for our wedding or honeymoon, both are good reminders why couples come together in the first place. Samantha
and Craig, the couple who created the "All the Guests Wore
White" wedding in Chapter 5, wanted their honeymoon to "enhance the dimensions already between us."

Like Padmini and Michael, they bring out the gypsy in each
other. Every summer for the eight years they lived together before marrying, the couple traveled to far-flung destinations.
Even though the pair were veterans of countless shared trips,
each knew this vacation would be special. "The honeymoon
did feel different because this time I was going away with my
husband," Samantha stated. "There was an added something,
a deepening."

Samantha and Craig knew they would need a short
breather before setting off on their high-culture honeymoon in

France, Holland, and Belgium. "We needed time to settle in and rest up after the crescendo of the wedding," Craig explained, "but we couldn't even do it in our own house!" Not only had they hosted their "nupital event" in their backyard, out-of-town guests had taken over their spare bedroom and den for a few days as well. So just to carve out some much needed space, avoid "business as usual," and recharge for their trip, the newlyweds retreated to a local hotel for two nights.

During the short lull between their wedding and honeymoon, the couple caught a fleeting case of the post-wedding bell blues. A solid year of thinking, planning, and talking "wedding" had dominated nearly all of their waking moments. "Now what?" echoed in the empty space. "But with Paris to look forward to," Samantha interjected, putting their mild gloom into perspective, "how bad of a letdown could it have been?" Soothing fine wines, soul-inspiring architecture, and museum after museum of fine art beckoned them—instant antidotes to their doldrums.

Certain aspects of their honeymoon—the major travel connections and big-city hotel reservations—had been confirmed in advance. But overplanning isn't Samantha and Craig's style. Stumbling onto this or bumping into that is. They both love just letting things happen.

Naturally, the epicurean delights of Europe didn't disappoint them. They wandered in and out of Gothic churches to their hearts' content, dined in the cobblestone courtyards of French country inns, and poked through flea markets held in medieval squares. Mostly, they found themselves flowing through these events rather than slavishly relying on guidebooks for what had to be seen or done. As a result, they pampered themselves with just the honeymoon they wanted: inspired, spontaneous, and brimming with the unexpected.

Honeymoons bring couples back to the "here and now" after months or more of being future-focused on the Wedding Day. Fiancés become consumed to the point of distraction with details: checklists, appointments, reservations, deposits, fittings, auditions, contracts, and so on. It is easy to lose sight of the present. So how do you find your way back?

Some swear by honeymoons that exercise the body and clear the mind. Those of this ilk may sign up for a short stint on an archaeological excavation in the Yucatan, book a bird-watching expedition in the Florida Everglades, or join a bicycling tour in Virginia's Blue Ridge Mountains just as the autumn leaves are turning.

Combining avocations with the healing properties of the Great Outdoors can do wonders for wedding-worn newlyweds. Of course an active honeymoon doesn't necessarily mean "roughing it," "slumming it," or "sweating it." Adventure traveling has become so sophisticated that you can pitch a tent while on safari in the Serengeti without giving up hot showers or a private toilet! Royal to rustic, a full range of outfitters are ready to accommodate you wherever and in whatever style you have become or would like to become accustomed to.

Neither Heidi nor Bruce (Chapter 6, "Remarrying with Children") aspired to luxury's lap, but launching their marriage amid untamed terrain without giving up the cozy comforts of home combined the best of both worlds. Their honeymoon itinerary: one week reconnoitering Glacier Bay and Icy Straits, Alaska. "We are nature-lovers and peak-experience freaks," Heidi said, grinning, her eyes widening with the memory, "so just the thought of us out there together stream fishing sounded like my definition of heaven!"

As a family, Heidi, Bruce, and Nathan go camping once every couple of months. Bruce's mountaineering skills are considerable, and he loved the idea of a wilderness honeymoon but wasn't ready to spend it chopping wood. When friends got wind of the couple's fantasy, a group of them set up an "Alaska or Bust Gift Registry." Their gift goal became paying for several nights at a hunting and fishing lodge, jumping-off point for flightseeing the Fairweather Mountain Range in a bush plane, kayaking overnight up the rugged fjords, and whale watching in Mid Bay. "Staying at a first-class inn with snow-capped mountains nearby and moose grazing outside our front door was the perfect mix," Bruce stated. "We got to enjoy all the grandeur without the grunge!"

For an entire week, after each "outdoorsy" day, the invigorated couple would return to their guest room and soak in a hot bath. Family-style meals of fresh-caught salmon or halibut took the place of campfire cookouts, but neither newlywed complained. Each glorious day seemed to outdo the one preceding it. "Bruce and I experienced things together in a week that few people ever see in a lifetime—calving icebergs, migrating Orca and humpback whales," Heidi reflected. "Sharing all that made us feel even closer."

Partaking in common interests and joint discoveries forge bonds and keep marriages vital and growing. A honeymoon is a time to both steep yourself in the present and make memories. But most of all, a honeymoon should be *fun*. And that can mean everything from "vegging-out" to venturing forth. Any kind of life-loving experience will do, as long as it involves the two of you.

Leaving the Kids Behind

But what if there are more than just the two of you to consider? Not every couple can just take off on a honeymoon and disappear into a cloud of nuptial bliss. Many of today's newlyweds have children to think of and plan for. Remarrying partners with children as well as never-before-married single parents are on the rise, and their honeymoons are affected by their concern for the children they leave behind.

In rare instances, a couple may opt for a "family honeymoon," which, technically speaking, doesn't qualify as a honeymoon at all. A family honeymoon is actually a family vacation that takes place after a wedding. Such a trip officially inaugurates the beginning of a blended family's life together. On the plus side, a good time together, right off the bat, can lessen children's initial uncertainties that they will be left out of the picture because of the new stepparent.

Naturally, a family honeymoon is workable only if *both* adults wholeheartedly endorse the idea and realize, up front, what they are in for. However, if one of the new spouses, probably the nonparent, hasn't bought in 100 percent, it's quite possible your family honeymoon could backfire. Count on the parent-spouse being hard-pressed to divide his or her time between a new mate and the child(ren). Even if child care is available at the vacation site so that the newlyweds can sneak away by themselves, stolen moments don't come close to the undivided attention that newlyweds enjoy on a child-free honeymoon. Chances are the dissenting spouse will feel shortchanged and resentful. As the days wear on, a honeymoon like this may begin to feel more and more as though you should have never left home.

For these reasons, most newlyweds with children opt for an adult-only honeymoon—time out to relish being alone together, far from the hectic and ever present demands of family life. A strong argument can be made that it's healthy for the children, as well. The honeymoon can be used to teach children that this is what grown-ups do when they first marry, and it is different from what families do when they go places together. Drawing this clear boundary encourages them to respect the autonomy and special nature of the married couple's relationship as something apart from being a mom, dad, or stepparent.

If leaving the children behind is your choice, then making provisions for their well-being during your absence turns on a number of factors, including the number of children involved, their ages, who has custody, the availability of child care, the length of the honeymoon, and the remoteness of your destination.

What can you do as a parent to prepare young children for what might be the longest period that they have ever been separated from you? Talking about your travel plans with your child is a first step. Heidi and Bruce showered Nathan with brochures from the Alaska inn and flagged the northernmost state for him on the map. The four-year-old also accompanied them to the sporting goods store where he helped select trail mix and other supplies for their day excursions.

Heidi's mother and father generously agreed to care for Nathan while they were gone. One big advantage is that Nathan is used to being in their care. He keeps clothes and toys at their house and they often pick him up from day care if Heidi or Bruce is working. Several days before their departure, the newlyweds made sure to ask Nathan what he wanted to take with him for his "sleep-over." Nathan decided on a glob of Play-Doh, two fire engines, and his biggest cannister of Legos. A new Winnie the Pooh toothbrush from Grandma and Grandpa was waiting for him in the bathroom when he arrived for the week.

Willing and able grandparents or relatives who live nearby are a godsend. Otherwise, finding quality child care for the duration of a honeymoon can be nearly impossible. It's an obstacle faced by many who don't have anyone close to rely on. "If my parents hadn't been able to take Nathan, I don't know what we would have done—cut our honeymoon down to two days or maybe cut it out altogether," Heidi said, thanking her lucky stars.

Another parental concern is ease of communication to home. With Nathan being so young, Heidi and Bruce wanted to be able to stay in touch if necessary. In a conversation before their arrival, the innkeepers assured them that the inn's telecommunications were state of the art. Phoning was no problem and as remote as Glacier Bay sounds, a round-trip jet from Juneau serves the area daily. The couple gave Nathan's grandparents the lodge's telephone number, but Nathan was so busy with his specially planned outings to the zoo, natural history museum, and the movies that he forgot to miss them. Not so for the honeymooners. "About midway through our honeymoon we missed Nathan so much that we called to tell him about everything we'd seen and done," Bruce told us. "He got the biggest kick hearing about the baby sea lions we'd seen."

By week's end, Bruce and Heidi were prepared to head home. They called Nathan on the day of their departure and told him they'd be picking him up the next morning. Before boarding the plane, they stopped at the airport curio shop and bought a souvenir for Nathan's stuffed animal collection: a baby sea lion for them all to remember Alaska.

Making childcare arrangements for an only child is hard enough, but what if you have more? Deborah and Greg, mom and dad of the Russell Bunch, are a good example of how caretaking concerns differ when the children are older and there are more of them: six to be exact, ranging from ages six to twelve. Way before the wedding, the couple informed their brood of their honeymoon. "They know people go away and they were fine about us leaving," Greg said with a chuckle, "but they kept on teasing us saying, 'Can we come? Can we come?' "

Absolutely Not! Deborah and Greg wanted their honeymoon all to themselves. On the evening of their wedding, the couple made a quick getaway and checked into the local airport hotel. By early the next morning they were on their way to Hawaii for ten days. Their anticipation was running high: never, over the course of their entire courtship, had the newlyweds ever spent much more than a day or two totally alone together.

For this and other reasons, their honeymoon started to look like Shangri-la. Deborah explained why. "The wedding was such a hectic time—pleasing everyone, pressure from ex's, the kids. Although I was up for the day of the wedding, I can remember a few days before sitting in the bathroom and just sobbing. As soon as we got to the hotel we both passed out from physical and emotional exhaustion!" Not an auspicious beginning, but the newlyweds made up for it.

Leaving six children behind took some maneuvering. Fortunately, there were helpful grandparents in the picture. In this case, the caretakers came to the children's house instead of the other way around. Transporting ten-days' worth of kid gear to their grandparents' home would have taken a Bekins moving van! Besides, they didn't have that many extra bedrooms. So the Russell Bunch stayed put.

To outsiders, the ratio of one set of grandparents to six grandchildren seems daunting. Potentially, yes. But Deborah and Greg, in addition to organizing their entire wedding, had grocery shopped beforehand and stocked both freezers and the double refrigerator with prepared dinners and enough food to feed an army, or at least their voracious family.

Another saving grace was that Deborah and Greg's children are old enough to entertain themselves, and there are enough of them to entertain each other. So while they still need supervision, they didn't need as much one-on-one attention as Heidi and Bruce's four-year-old Nathan. The grandparents were also spared the daily task of chauffeuring the children back and forth to their schools, because Deborah and Greg's honeymoon took place during summer vacation.

Meanwhile, on the beaches of Maui, Deborah and Greg were soaking up the peace and tranquillity they so thoroughly deserved. Did they worry about anyone on the mainland? Not once, knowing that they were in trusted hands. Like Heidi and Bruce, Deborah and Greg lugged back a suitcase full of trinkets for everyone, T-shirts, beach towels, lots of pictures, and an especially nice gift for the grandparents, who had truly gone beyond the call of duty. Deborah and Greg's own homecoming committee greeted them upon their return. In a gleeful chorus, all six children gathered round the newlyweds with hugs and kisses and welcomed them back home.

Early and Late Honeymoons

Reversing the order of the honeymoon from post-wedding to prewedding or delaying it for a considerable period are other options available to about-to-be-married couples. If you can live with the anticlimactic feelings of having to go home after the wedding, either choice has its advantages.

One good thing about scheduling a honeymoon before your big event is that you get to have fun *before* you get too tired to have any. So much goes into planning a wedding that by the processional a bride and groom are often running on pure adrenaline. After the rush, there's the crash. Count on it! Many a newlywed couple spend their wedding night conked out and the rest of their honeymoon recuperating from utter exhaustion.

Another advantage of taking a honeymoon ahead of time is that you arrive back on your wedding scene refreshed and relaxed. No small accomplishment, by the way. As a tonic to frayed nerves; a time-out to tune in to yourself, your spouse-to-be, and the reasons why you are marrying, prehoneymoons are ideal. But, they have their limits. As you may recall, Amy and Doug's combination Caribbean honeymoon + ceremony was blissful, but they couldn't escape forever. Whatever unfinished business they left behind—from last-minute reception details to family tiffs—awaited their return just like everyone else. Regrettably, honeymoons aren't a permanent fix, just a temporary respite—no matter when you take them.

Charlotte and David, from Chapter 3, the couple who bootlegged their small ceremony in the garden of a grand hotel, took a prehoneymoon for practical reasons. Charlotte was starting a new job the day after the wedding, and David was scheduled for a series of dental surgeries.

Even though this was honeymoon number three for both of them, Charlotte and David were looking forward to their romantic interlude with the same anticipation as if it were their first. The two are so much in love that simply being together took precedence over elaborate honeymoon plans. Besides, Charlotte's first honeymoon, years earlier, had been a six-week whirlwind tour of Europe, hauling tons of luggage, dressing formally for dinner, door-to-door service—the whole works. Delight soon turned to drudgery. Then and there, she swore off any future travel dictated by prepaid reservations and prearranged schedules.

David's suggestion that they take a weeklong drive up the coast with no specific itinerary sounded ideal. "We let the car kind of take us," Charlotte remembered. "We'd get lost and find places that we never intended to find that were better than the places we were looking for." Over the course of their thousand-mile trip they never even listened to the radio. Instead, they passed hours silently drinking in the countryside with their eyes or engaging in effortless conversation. "To me, that says something about how easy we feel together," she said knowingly.

Being reminded of how good of a "fit" you are with your prospective mate is very reassuring. In those dark, fleeting moments before the wedding when you are wondering if you're making the right choice, a glorious prehoneymoon can reaffirm all the reasons why you have. "Our trip before the wedding was the cement that held everything together because we knew how we felt . . . about so many things," David observed.

Jayn and Jeff, the "Not-So-Great Lakes Getaway" bride and groom of Chapter 7, concurred, but for different reasons. This couple's Washington Island wedding was mired in mishaps and miscalculations. The reservoir of good feelings they'd accumulated during their honeymoon some three months before, buoyed their failing spirits and hedged their disappointments when almost nothing turned out the way they expected. Being able to remember the elation they felt on their honeymoon provided much-needed reminders that their marriage wasn't doomed just because the wedding plans seemed to be.

More important, the "real wedding," as far as Jeff was concerned, had already taken place before Washington Island. "We like to think we got married on our honeymoon," he told us. "We bought these sterling silver wedding bands in an alley jewelry shop in Heidelberg and put them on, then and there." From that moment on, the deed was done. In their minds, the wedding to come was just a formality.

What Jeff went on to say applies in some way to every couple who decides to marry. "You don't need the world looking at you or listening to you to know you are married, it is a private feeling the two of you share, and that can happen any-where!"

On the other side of the honeymoon spectrum are new-lyweds who delay the momentous trip until their energy, finances, or schedules permit. For many who hold full-time jobs, taking this day and that day off to tend to wedding plans eats into the same vacation time that might very well count toward the honeymoon. By the time the honeymoon rolls around, you may have to cut into your sick days or ar-range for leave without pay. This was one reason why Ben and Diane (Chapter 8) spent their honeymoon in the British Isles a year and a half after they married. "All told we spent be-tween five to ten working days planning the wedding and that doesn't even count the hours I spent on the phone at work making wedding-related calls," Ben told us.

Delaying the honeymoon also served another purpose: tak-ing the pressure off. Expectations soar at the whisper of the word "honeymoon." We imagine only the most divine respite, with every detail falling into place like clockwork: flawlessly executed travel arrangements, perfect weather, fun-filled days, passion-filled nights. The vacation to top all vacations. Ulti-mate perfection in every way. Even though these are impossi-bly high standards to wish for, the myth of the honeyspun honeymoon is hard to resist. Few newlyweds try.

But not Ben and Diane. "There are too many expectations about honeymoons," Ben lamented, "and I didn't want to take one where we'd be under pressure to create a world of perfec-tion." Although more romantically inclined than Ben, Diane wasn't prepared to leap into vacation mode immediately after-ward either. The mere thought of planning anything else, espe-cially her honeymoon, on the heels of the wedding was too overwhelming. Not only had the festivities and entertaining out-of-town guests left her with zero physical energy, she didn't feel up to it emotionally. "It would have felt artificial to have packed up and gone away right away, but maybe a vacation would have helped me out of my postnuptial depression."

Forcing themselves to honeymoon just because that's what newlyweds automatically do immediately following a wedding seemed to inflate the stakes even more, especially since they weren't *ready* to take one. So Ben and Diane waited until they were. When the timing was right, the newlyweds threw themselves into the pleasure of honeymoon planning with renewed enthusiasm. And while Ben still preferred to think of the trip as a vacation, and Diane, a honeymoon, once they got around to it they had an utterly smashing time.

Sometimes honeymoons are delayed more for reasons of "where to go" than "when to go." What do you do if your new mate wants to outward-bound and you just want to cocoon? You have five basic options (1) do both—if you are equally gracious and have the time and the money; (2) chance it— toss a coin and hope for the best; (3) cave in—if you do, the next vacation choice is yours; (4) compromise—agree on a third destination; or (5) throw your fates to the wind—pick a destination out of a hat. But, whatever you do, *go somewhere!* Don't skip the honeymoon just because you're having trouble deciding where to take it.

Leslie and Mark's three-day mini-honeymoon—one day before, during, and after the wedding—was a stopgap measure until they could take their bona fide honeymoon four months later. Because the newlyweds hadn't lived together prior to marriage, the postponement gave them an opportunity to adjust emotionally to merging their lives.

Nor did the delay take anything away from the "ceremonial significance" of the trip. "Our honeymoon was perfectly timed," Mark explained. "After the first months of getting used to each other, taking off gave us a chance to unjangle our nerves and reaffirm why we got married in the first place!"

If timing wasn't a problem, where to honeymoon was. Leslie wanted to go to Martha's Vineyard for two weeks—no phones, no people; Mark wanted to go backpacking—no beds, no people. "It sounds corny," said Leslie, "but, just like planning the wedding, you have to take each other into consideration. Mark likes adventure and I lean more toward relaxation."

Although they never did agree on the definitive honeymoon destination, a prior commitment helped them make up their minds. Long before they'd set their wedding date, Leslie and Mark had signed up with several members of their yoga class to attend a one-week retreat in Hawaii. By the time honeymoon ideas were being discussed, combining it with the retreat didn't seem like such a bad plan. Dovetailing the two would save on airfare, travel time, and hassles.

The newlyweds came to a compromise: one week alone in a rented house on the north shore of Oahu followed by one week at the yoga retreat with friends, pursuing their joint interest. It was a "give a little; get a little" proposition. Leslie would have to return to the place where she had honeymooned with her first husband some years before, but at least she would have a relaxing vacation. Mark would have to give up his idea of an adventure, but at least they'd be alone, together, in a secluded setting, close to nature.

Ideal or no, the honeymoon, in Leslie's words, was still "precious and intense." Aptly put, since Mark was back on the road for seven weeks upon their return home. But now that their appetite has been whetted, "the ideal honeymoon" is on the drawing boards. "I can imagine it would be nice to take a honeymoon after a year of marriage," Mark mused. A split second later, Leslie raised him one. "What about every year!" she said, with yearning and wisdom in her voice.

Once and Only Once

As enchanting as the idea of a recurring honeymoon is, the unsentimental truth is that you get one, and only one, honeymoon per marriage. A married couple can look forward to years of romantic weekend getaways, holiday vacations, and recreational travel, but the *first* time away as husband and wife is special. Here's why.

Typically, a honeymoon takes place immediately following a

wedding and before settling down to married life. This in-between time symbolically represents the transition of newly-weds from an unmarried to a married state. Taking their leave punctuates the end of the newlyweds' single status. Returning marks a beginning, an entry into shared life and a new role. A life threshold has been crossed . . . the future is approaching.

There are other reasons why a honeymoon is special. It is one of the rare times we're encouraged to indulge ourselves, to take our dream vacation, to let ourselves go. A honeymoon is a chance to loaf, make love, act on whims, laugh, experiment, and wallow in happiness. A private festival of intimacy devoted exclusively to each other. A celebration of our spontaneous, playful, and relaxed selves—the best of who we are.

More than the honeymoon suite, more than the meals you eat or the landmarks you visit, a honeymoon is the total essence of what it is like *being* together, moment to moment and loving it. If planning a wedding teaches a bride and groom some of the preliminary lessons of marriage, then a honeymoon can remind newlyweds of the more ephemeral ones, especially upon your return to real life, real pressures, and real problems. As a touchstone for the essential spark between you and your mate, there is nothing as precious.

Honeymoon Tips

1. Don't overplan your honeymoon. An overambitious travel itinerary can be as taxing as an overambitious wedding.

2. If you've already been living together for months or years and you want your honeymoon to have a special sexual edge, abstain from lovemaking a week or two prior to your wedding. Store up the anticipation for your postnuptial holiday.

3. Take the pressure off. If you expect your honeymoon to be one peak experience after another, you may be setting yourself up for disappointment. The surest way to prevent a peak experience is to expect one.

4. Surprise and delight each other with small gifts, unexpected detours, and unplanned activities.

5. Do at least one thing together that you've never done before.

6. There's no rule that says you have to spend every second together on your honeymoon to prove your love. If you want to go shopping and she wants to go horseback riding, don't feel guilty about taking a break from each other for a few hours.

7. Spare yourself fights about finances on your honeymoon by deciding ahead of time how much you want to spend, setting aside a "splurge fund," and spending it with abandon.

8. If you are a newlywed parent, it's probably best to leave your contact number with the caretaker, not with the child(ren). Otherwise, you may be besieged with calls demanding the immediate answers to such pressing questions as: Where did you put my roller skates? or Can I spend the rest of my allowance on a Ron Gant rookie card?

9. Tell the hotel and restaurant staff you're honeymooning. They'll probably treat you to special niceties such as a complimentary bottle of champagne, a luscious fruit basket, or a bouquet of fresh flowers for your room.

10. Remember that the most valuable honeymoon souvenir cannot be packed in a suitcase, noted in a diary or captured on video. It's the feeling that the two of you have access to your own private world—no matter what crowded planet you live on.

Miscellaneous Creative Wedding Ideas

Alternatives to Showers, Stag Parties and Rehearsal Dinners

1. **"Coed Recipe Dinner Party"**

   Guests are asked to write (and illustrate, if they're artistically inclined) their favorite recipe on an attractive card and give it to the party host or hostess who places them all in a Friends Cookbook. The friends then bring the same culinary concoction to a prenuptial potluck dinner. In addition to sampling their guests' offerings, the bride and groom will receive the Friends Cookbook as a lasting tribute to their marriage, their friends, and good food. (Recipe cards can also include marital advice, well wishes, romantic philosophy, and such.)

2. **"Bride Versus Groom Baseball Game"**

   Start a wedding league of your own with "blushing bride" and "gushing groom" T-shirts for each team and a picnic brunch after the big game. Who says prewedding parties can't be athletic?

3. **"Where We Met" or "Where We Went on Our First Date Party"**

Whether it was a hot-dog stand, a rock concert, the gym, or a five-star restaurant, pay homage to your romantic roots by hosting a prewedding party there with your closest family and friends.

4. **"Separate but Equal Camping Trips"**

There's something to be said for one-sex-only gatherings: they're fun. But a lot of us feel traditional stag parties and ladies' luncheons are as outdated as the LP and 45. How about this for an update: a prewedding weekend camp-out segregated by sex? As an option, campsites could be close by so everyone can get together on the last night . . .

Create Your Own Officiant

If you'd like your ceremony performed by someone you respect and feel close to—but you're not affiliated with any particular religion and don't want to be married by a judge—consider having a friend, relative, therapist, or other wise person become "ordained" by the Universal Life Church. It's a simple process that involves filling out a form and paying a nominal fee, after which the person who applies is legally entitled to perform marriage ceremonies. Contact Universal Life Church, 6415 Sunset Rd., Joshua Tree, CA 92252; 800-446-9351.

Beyond Pots and Pans Gift Registries

The housewares section of your local department store is *not* the only source for potential wedding gifts. If you've already outfitted two households and don't need another salad bowl or coffeemaker, consider the alternatives:

1. Home and Garden Centers

    Sign up to receive power tools, mini blinds, lawn chairs, or rose bushes.

2. Sporting Goods Stores

    Camping gear, tennis rackets, golf balls, barbells. Start your marriage off equipped!

3. Music/Video Stores

    Register for the complete works of Elvis Costello . . . or Bette Davis.

4. Bookstores

    List either specific titles or general subject categories for gift givers to choose from.

5. Travel Agencies

    Wedding well-wishers can contribute to your honeymoon or the trip you want to take *after* the honeymoon.

6. Our First Home Registry

    A special bank account can be designated for all cash gifts . . . to go directly toward a down payment on a home mortgage. With today's real estate prices, helping a couple achieve this dream is a gift of a lifetime!

Other Novel Wedding Gift Ideas

Designate a friend as your "wedding gift consultant" so people can contact him or her for unusual ideas that have your stamp of approval, such as:

1. Gift certificates: for restaurants, unisex clothing stores, spas (for a double massage and mineral bath).

2. Tickets: to concerts, plays, museums, hockey games . . .

3. One big item (as opposed to a lot of unneeded small things): have your "wedding gift consultant" organize contributions toward purchase of a refrigerator, a Persian rug, an original artwork.

4. In-kind services: Personal "certificates" for child care, a home-cooked dinner party for four, or one-day's help painting a room in a new house.

5. X number of days of housecleaning services to be arranged at the newlyweds' discretion. With so many wedding details to worry about, everyday chores often go by the wayside. What a luxury to have someone else tidy up either just prior to the wedding day and/or while the newlyweds are honeymooning.

6. A monthly delivery of fresh flowers for the duration of one year: from Wedding Day to First Anniversary.

7. Donations to your favorite charities or nonprofit organizations.

Index